"Say Cheese!"

The Youth

'Must', will',
'shall', 'can'
must be your
positive verbs
and not 'if'!

Swami Chinmayananda in Houston, U.S.A. 1991.

The youth
are not useless.
They are
used less!

"Say Cheese!"
Witty Wisdom

by Swami Chinmayananda

Photographs and Cartoons
by Anjali Singh

© Central Chinmaya Mission Trust

First Edition: August   2004   -   7000   copies
Reprint   October   2006   -   3000   copies

Published by:
CENTRAL CHINMAYA MISSION TRUST
Sandeepany Sadhanalaya
Saki Vihar Road,
Mumbai - 400 072, INDIA.
Tel.: 91-22-28572367 / 28575806
Fax: 91-22-28573065
Email: ccmt@vsnl.com
Website: www.chinmayamission.com

Distribution Centre in USA:
CHINMAYA MISSION WEST
Publications Division,
560 Bridgetown Pike,
Langhorne, PA 19053, USA.
Tel: (215) 396-0390
Fax: (215) 396-9710
Email: publications@chinmaya.org
Website: www.chinmayapublications.org

Printed by:
SAGAR UNLIMITED
Unit No. 1, YAC Industrial Estate,
Kondivita Lane, Andheri Kurla Road,
Andheri (E), Mumbai - 400 059.
Tel.: 28362777 / 28227699

Book and Cover Design:
Ramona Sood, ramona@cafedreams.com

Price: Rs. 150/-

ISBN 81-7597-246-7

Contents

Preface

This book introduces the Science of Life, Vedanta, with wit and logic. Its target audience is the youth. Both wit and logic were hallmarks of the great Vedantic teacher, Swami Chinmayananda, whose images and words we have captured in this publication.

Swami Chinmayananda's ready wit in the photographic section is a reflection of his personality as a keen observer, ever alert, full of laughter and quick repartee. The words in the photographs were said by him at some point in time to someone in particular or to a general audience, but not necessarily to the person in the photograph.

The photographs appear as originally shot, with the place and year indicated in the bottom line. Only two pictures, "Ocean of Change" and "Legacy", are digital combinations. Cartoons have been superimposed on some photographs, and photographs on some cartoons.

The commentary section has been collected in various bits from books, talks, and letters of Swami Chinmayananda and ordered according to topic.

The idea for this book came from **Swami Chidananda**, President of the Divine Life Society, Rishikesh, when he was looking for an inspiring booklet to send to a young man. "Why doesn't Chinmaya Mission make a book with some 'sparkles' in it?" he suggested.

The idea progressed further when Swami Mitrananda of Chinmaya Mission was speaking in Delhi on the lives of saints, and while speaking of **Sadhu Vaswani**, he said that Sadhu Vaswani did not like being photographed, but had to concede when a photograph was required for his passport. "Don't move, or it will blur!" Sadhu Vaswani had said to the photographer. His sentence, with its underlying deep message, was reminiscent of a similar conversation I had had with my guru, Swami Chinmayananda, while taking his photograph in Taiwan. "Don't move, Swamiji!" I had said, and he had replied: "I never do!" - reminding me that an immovable Essence defines the true nature of each one of us. Remembering his answer sparked the idea for this book.

continued overleaf...

Higher Vision!

If one looks at each photograph in this book (or anything else in life, for that matter) in the light of Vedanta, it will portray an inspiring vision, and if one looks at it light-heartedly, it will portray humour. If one looks at it with both viewpoints combined, it will be seen to portray wisdom laced with engaging wit. One's view of life can be happy or sad, dull or inspiring. This whole book is about changing one's vision of life to embrace joy and unity, and Swamiji shows us how!

Our thanks to **Swami Swaroopananda, Swami Mitrananda**, and to the Chyks (Chinmaya Yuva Kendra) from Chennai, Hyderabad, Bangalore and Delhi, who contributed many of the witty comments of Swamiji that they had overheard; and to Geeta Nanda for enthusiastically typing the entire commentary section.

Swami Tejomayananda, the head of Chinmaya Mission, liked the annotated photographs when they were seen displayed as a photographic exhibition in 2001 in Mumbai. Without hesitation he said "Yes" to the suggestion that the collection come out as a book for the youth. Others are welcome to enjoy it too.

— **Anjali Singh**

This is what Swami Tejomayananda wrote after seeing the manuscript:

ॐ

Beautiful Book..
A must for youth
of all times.

Tejomayananda

P.S. #1 With six swamis involved with the generation of this book – youth, your luck is in! In addition, Mata Brahmajyoti from Uttarkashi liked the concept of this book so much, that she has suggested that we publish it in Hindi as well. That adds up to seven swamis' blessings.

P.S. #2 Moral: Blessings count!

To a Gynaecologist

You deliver into this world; I deliver out of this world!

Swami Chinmayananda speaking to a visitor in 1985 during a heart check up in a hospital in New Jersey, U.S.A.

For further reading: Religion and Human Values by Swami Chinmayananda
Hindu Culture by Swami Tejomayananda
Why do we? by Swamini Vimalananda

Religion – its Utility

Religion is a great science, and it has a glorious utility in the world. We are not referring to the religion of ringing-the-bells. We are referring to that aspect of religion, that helps us to discover in oneself, a new strength and vitality to face one's challenges in life.

Religion is the technique of perfect living, a process which brings forth an effective personality out of even a shattered man of despairs and disappointments.

Handle with Care!

About time!

Swami Chinmayananda in Vienna, Austria, 1982.

3

The Purpose of Life

Every unicellular organism in life is breeding. So what is it so spectacular that you are doing?

The religious text books prescribe certain laws of living, which define for us the modes of contact with the world of objects around us, so that we may have a more harmonious and dynamic existence. Philosophy and religion rehabilitate man's personality and provide him with the necessary equilibrium to make his inner life more meaningful.

For instance, one has the freedom to use electricity in his home in any manner he chooses. To establish a correct relationship with it, one has to follow the laws of electricity, or else the same power can mercilessly destroy him. To condemn religious precepts as shackles put upon man's natural freedom is to misunderstand the purpose of religion.

The inability to distinguish between freedom and licence is at the root of modern man's aversion to religion. An intelligent and proper understanding of the laws governing man's inner personality, inspires pursuits of higher ideals and gives him a broad vision of life, and an equipoise to face the vicissitudes of life.

All of us are seeking happiness because happiness is the real Self of man, his natural state of being. Religion shows us the direction in which to find it.

For further reading: Art of Living: Chapters 1 & 2 by Swami Chinmayananda
The Game of Life by Swami Tejomayananda

The Existence of God

I have got this whole idea of God sorted out! If there is a God, he is going to be too nice to want to punish me no matter how I act..... Right? And if there isn't any God, then I haven't really lost anything!

Swami Chinmayananda in San Jose, California, U.S.A. 1983.

Demystifying God

Our age has been branded as atheistic and secular because we dare to question and we do so openly. Since faith has the least hold on us, Vedanta* - as expounded in the Upanishads - has a compelling charm. **Hinduism is not the declaration of any one individual,** but is the conclusion of generations of investigators. The investigators, our great *rishis* or sages, found that the subtlest of the subtle, the principle, or truth, resides within us, a divine spark enveloped *as it were* by the grosser coatings of matter, the grossest being the physical body.

The sum total of all the intellects of all the individuals (*jivas*) that are living in the visible world (*jagat*) is the concept of God. Not our conception of God as Rama, Krishna, Siva, Christ, Mohammed etc., but the total concept, the God principle. The particular incarnations are only manifestations of the God-principle. **God is the total causal body of the universe.**

Take the example of *cotton*, from which *thread* came and reshaped into *cloth* with all its patterns. The principle of truth is like cotton. From truth an immediate modification is the God-principle (thread) called Ishwara, and the modification of the God-principle is man (cloth). In Vedanta, the all pervading Supreme Reality does not actually undergo any change, as milk changes to curd. **All plurality is only an appearance like a rope mistaken for a snake.** Appearance is time bound. God-principle is beyond time.

Be at peace with God, whatever you conceive Him to be.

*The science of life that underlies all religions

The Empiricist!

Gravitation Force: 32ft. per second, per second...

Is Seeing Believing?

Earth is round
Earth moves
Not seen but true

Sky is blue
Sunset is golden
Seen but false

Energy in the atom
Vitality in the sun
Gravitational force
Not seen but true

Double moon
Mirage waters
Dream and hallucinations
Seen but false

World we see, but not true.
Truth we see not, but true

Further reading: Kena Upanishad commentary by Swami Chinmayananda

The need for a Guru

9

The Need for a Guru

The very fact that you are asking these questions clearly shows that we need teachers to teach us. Is there anything we do well with confidence, or any amount of mastery that has not been taught to us? If, **for every perfect act in the world in any activity, we need the guidance of an instructor,** we can well understand the need for a *guru* in the spiritual path; for there we have to deal with the subtlest forces and the enormous confusions of the vehicle called the mind, and with its moods called delusions.

The *guru*-disciple relationship is unavoidable. **Every great master has been under the guidance of a teacher. It is not true to say that one can reach the goal just through books.** A teacher is necessary. The teacher's job is to nurture the student with right thoughts, but the blossoming – the fragrance of the personality - must come from within the student.

How does one choose a *guru*? It is not a question of the disciple selecting the guru. He gravitates towards a *guru*, and he will find exactly the *guru* he needs for his present state of mental development. So, choose whatever *guru* comes to you, but understand that the only *guru* is He, the Lord, who expresses in many forms. We revere and worship the Lord as manifesting through the individual. No individual mortal is ever a preceptor. **The Lord alone is the teacher, everywhere, at all times.**

The most important thing is our own self effort. Keep purifying the mind and the *guru* necessary for our next stage of growth shall reach us. This is the eternal law. Hour by hour, the world around us is so ordered, as to give us the necessary dosage of experiences. **When we come to deserve a master, he shall reach us.** Be good, be kind, be sincere.

There is almost an enchantment of unbelievable magic in the method of communication adopted by nature in guiding seekers.

Further reading: Mananam:The Essential Teacher, page 10.
Katha Upanishad : verse 5, commentary by Swami Chinmayananda

The Goal

The Goal

It is very necessary to discover a great purpose or goal in life. Having gained that goal or ideal, for which you have concentrated all your education – apply yourself to it, whether it be political or economic. It should be an ideal that you have chosen according to your heart, not an ideal that somebody has given you, but that which appeals to you the most – then from it, a new enthusiasm comes to you. When there is enthusiasm, then sincerity, ardour and consistency of purpose automatically follow and a new column of energy arises in you.

The goal has to be something higher than your self, your family and worldly comfort. If there is a social vision that moves us forward, we discover within ourselves a new source of energy. **If our head and heart are working where the hands are working, there comes the artistic perfection.**

Do not allow this energy to be dissipated in the futile memories of the past, regrets of failures, the imagined sorrows of the future, or in the excitement of the present.

Thus, bring your entire energy focused into activity. That is the highest creative action.

Where the physical, mental and intellectual personalities become integrated, the individual is nearer to perfection.

When an individual has discovered new energy within himself, has learnt the art of stopping the dissipation, has learnt the art of fixing the entire energy to the piece of work in hand, a great joy called 'the joy of the artisan' starts welling up in the mind. The joy of the artisan can be understood only when you experience it.

If we know how to turn our vision in the right direction to which we surrender our work, then even typing, which is considered to be a dreary work, can give us our dividend of joy. **It matters not *what* we do, but the glory of endeavour lies in *how* we do it.**

continued....

From the Womb to the Tomb!

Swami Chinmayananda in Melbourne, Australia 1987.

13

We can discover our joy in the precision and perfection of the work that we turn out. Whether others recognize it or not, we get satisfaction that we did our work as best as we could. **The quality of action depends upon the ideals which guide and inspire an individual.** A person with no ideals feels fatigued in his work. This fatigue is caused by the strain and stress which we invite, by craving for indulgence in sense objects and ceaseless expectation of the fruits of our actions.

The secret of success, therefore, **lies in activities undertaken with a spirit of surrender to an ideal.**

Be firm in your determination to reach out and gain your goal. Be tireless in your efforts to get at what you have planned to win. Never hesitate... never vacillate, or doubt your ability to storm your goal. That will be a miserable life. It is thereafter, but a spider's life: to live in suspense! Be prepared to meet any trouble, and march smoothly to your goal. Why hesitate when the Lord is with you, at your elbow ever to help you.

History is full of instances, wherein, victory would have been to the vanquished, if only they had battled a little longer! We often fail for lack of perseverance in our efforts. We leave our work half done in our impatience. **Every job demands its quota of efforts**. Never give up too soon. Strive on until you win.

For further reading: Geeta Chapter III commentary by Swami Chinmayananda
Art of Man Making by Swami Chinmayananda

Striving for Excellence

For further reading:
The Holy Geeta Chapter III on Karma Yoga
Secret of Action by Swami Chinmayananda
Towards greater Success by Swami Tejomayananda
Secret of Success (in Hindi) by Swami Tejomayananda
Wealth Management by Swami Swaroopananda
Conscious Living by Swami Ishwarananda

CD's & Audio Cassettes:

Managing the Manager by Swami Swaroopananda
Wealth Management by Swami Swaroopananda
CEO by Swami Swaroopananda
Stress Management by Swami Nikhilananda

Video Cassettes:

Dexterity in Action by Swami Chinmayananda
On Excellence by Swami Chinmayananda
Value Based Management by Swami Chinmayananda
How to Win by Swami Chinmayananda

Striving for Excellence

There should be concentration in the work undertaken. If you cannot execute the work because your mind is clogged, your effort will be wasted. The clogging dissipates the dynamism.

There are **three causes** for the dissipation of mental energy:

1) **regrets of the past**
2) **anxieties for the future**
3) **excitements in the present**

The mind can be liberated from these clutches by surrendering itself at an altar, a goal or an ideal. Once having surrendered the results of an action to the altar of your dedication, be it God or the nation or a profession, the results no longer belong to you. ***The action becomes an act of worship.***

In this surrender, you have surrendered your anxieties and fears, so the work will come out efficiently. Your work will have quality, beauty, fragrance and perfection. You too will become a genius. This is called ***Karma Yoga.***

Self-effacement is the secret of inspiration. A genius at work is he who has established a perfect identity of his own mind and intellect with the work in hand. The best can come out of an orator or a painter or a sculptor or a musician or a writer, only when he forgets himself and gets lost in the work at hand.

The success and beauty of an individual life contributes to the glory and effectiveness of a nation.

Everyone with knowledge, exerts, sweats and toils. But only a few succeed in life. They generally forget that the mind is the "doer" in us, and the body is but our tool. **Learn to bring your mind where your hands are working**. Then see the results! Actions become excellent, and success is the tribute life pays to excellence.

Across the ocean of 'change'

Swami Chinmayananda with oar in hand, in Newport News in Virginia, U.S.A. 1985.
Swami Tejomayananda in Sidhbari, India. 1997. Photograph by Nanki Singh.

Leap from the shores of duality into the rigged boat of discrimination and ply ceaselessly towards the Horizon of Experience. Let the helmsman be 'shraddha' and keep the boat steady towards the Pole-star, the 'Mahavakya'. Carefully navigate around the dangerous rocks of your own lower nature. You shall reach the Eternal Haven of Peace and Bliss : TRUTH.

Drowned – Coated, Suited, Booted!

Life is not and should not be one constant steady flow; and when you see dark clouds gathering and storms threatening to burst out, you need not despair and leave the boat. Be steady at the helm of truth and steer steadily on the path of safety, which the *rishis* have chalked out for us. Constantly referring to the magnetometer of the inner purity, self-ward, gaze and go ahead... full steam, full speed.

Guru is the person who can guide you across the ocean of *change* (known as *bhavsaagar*), in which the shark of *samsar* is ever ready to swallow you. ***Samsar* is compared to a shark because the shark will not eat you limb by limb. It will swallow you whole – suit and boot.** The digestion takes place without your knowledge, even when you are living inside. In the chambers of the belly you can walk about. You can. You can go to the office, you can eat, sleep and breed and the digestive secretions will slowly work upon you and reduce you to a deplorable state of tension and stresses of life created by the ego and the endless avarices of the flesh. Are we not living death in the belly of *samsar*?

Get into the boat divine and end your struggles in the mid-ocean against the tumultuous, unending buffers. Once you have got into the boat, Chinmaya is your devoted nurse to serve you back to health and vigour. **This sadhu shall see you home. This is a solemn promise.**

Waiting for the audience!

Swami Chinmayananda and Swami Swaroopananda before a morning class in Taipei, Taiwan. 1987.

So great is the ignorance of human nature
that it does not realize the greatness of its ignorance.

The Vedantic Method

Listening is the first step in the ascent to the divine. The strategy of the veiling power of *tamas,* or inertia, is met and defeated by the Vedantic practice of listening called *sravana.*

The second stage is **reflection** called *mananam.* Here the agitations of the mind get controlled and a person gains a fair control over his senses.

In the third stage called *nidhidyasan,* the **contemplation** flights are higher and a person's intensity of concentration is more pointed and firm. A seeker slowly comes to manifest a certain amount of divinity and godliness at this stage.

Life is defined as a series of continuous experiences. If his experiences are happy, his life is happy.

Every experience is constituted of three essential factors: the **experiencer,** the **object of experience** and the relationship binding the two called **experiencing.** The subjective scientists confine their enquiry to the realm of the experiencer, who functions with four layers of his personality, and each personality layer has its own value and demands.

For further reading:
Art of Living: Chapter 10 by Swami Chinmayananda
Kindle Life by Swami Chinmayananda
Vivekchoodamani by Adi Sankara. Commentary by Swami Chinmayananda
Self-Unfoldment by Swami Chinmayananda

The Way and the Goal

Return back to the road by which from the Supreme you reached here and realize your own Self!

Swami Chinmayananda enroute Uttarkashi, India 1985.

Gradual Steps

Our seers have discovered a very attractive and pleasant looking path to help us get established on the road to reality.

The right conduct in life can be determined only when the individual has correct knowledge of **what has to be pursued** and **what is to be avoided.** The grand road to truth is the same for all. It cannot be determined by each pilgrim, according to his own whims and fancies. Scriptures are declared by those who had travelled the road many a time. The Scriptures are the reports left for our guidance, by those who successfully walked the 'path' earlier.

A correct knowledge and a clear intellectual vision of the goal and the direction in which it lies, and the possible difficulties en route, are the pre-requisites for the traveller. And when the *rishis* supply us with a map of the road-to-perfection, we, the humble pedestrians, must pursue the path faithfully and come to bless ourselves.

Study of the Scriptures in a spirit of total participation, augmented with frequent listening to the learned exponents, and a few direct contacts with the authentic masters is found to be very helpful in the beginning.

While listening we only **_participate_** in spiritual life. When we study, we get **_involved_** with the ideas to which we have listened. By repeating a mantra with or without a rosary, *mala,* and continuously fixing our mind on its divine import, we become *quiet and alert,* and in meditation we get **_committed_** to our ideal.

Self-control is not practised to kill the individuality in us, but to add to its tempo in performance, to its daring in vision, and to its brilliance in achievement.

The B.M.I. Chart

My P.F.T. tells my B.M.I. it's time to E.A.T.

ॐ =The infinite Reality, when it expresses through **V**= Vasanas, the psychological tendencies and identifies with **B.M.I.**= the body, mind and intellect, the instruments of perception, it becomes the limited **P.F.T.**= the perceiver, feeler, thinker, the sense of individuality in man. The PFT functions in the world of **O.E.T.**= the objects, emotions, and thoughts, the field of experience.

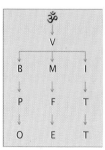

The Human Personality

The body, mind and intellect, **BMI,** are the **'tools'** that have their own distinct characters in each person, and the personality expressed when life throbs through them, is therefore distinct.

The world of experiences is made up of the world of objects, the world of emotional feelings and the world of ideas. All these put together is one's total **'field of experience'** called **OET.**

So then, one must know the art of tuning these instruments, the BMI, properly, so that through them one may have a full and proper experience of the world, to gain the joy of real existence in rediscovering the true nature of the experiencer that we consider as the perceiver, feeler, thinker, the **PFT,** the sense of **individuality** in man.

V stands for the *vasanas,* which makes a personality distinct. *Vasanas* are **psychological tendencies, repressions** and **suppressions**, buried in the unconscious layer of our personality, which is even beneath our subconscious layer. They give direction to our actions and are three in number - *sattvic, rajasic* and *tamasic* - the pure, the agitated and the dull. The *tamasic vasanas* can be removed by cultivating *rajasic vasanas* and *rajasic* can be ended by replacing them with *sattvic* ones. When the mind gets purer, even *sattvic vasanas* get exhausted and the divine Self shines forth vividly.

ॐ or **Om** is made up of three sound symbols **A-U-M** and the underlying silence. Om represents the **past, present and future**; the world of **waking, dream** and **deep sleep**; the **physical, emotional/intellectual** and **causal**; and the fourth is the **silence**, the substratum of sound. Om not only indicates the **spiritual centre in the individual** but also represents the **total spiritual reality** behind the delusory concept of the world of plurality. This denominator or factor which is the common experiencer in three fields of one's activity, is **the common I** – the eternal factor, the pure consciousness. The **Om** symbol is not only **an idol representing the absolute reality,** but it also represents the **relative reality.**

continued....

Deep Sleep State!

Om is a sound symbol representing the **fundamental truth,** the ultimate, eternal, **all pervading conscious principle**. The entire world cognized by our forefathers, by ourselves and our children **in the three periods of time,** is represented by Om. Om is the **substratum** for all that is limited in time and all that is not conditioned by it.

Om is the name of my own Self - **my true name**. Om chanting is very beneficial for all.

To transcend the three states is to break the greatest of the idols, Om itself. But Om is glorified as the super-most, as it is the immediate conveyer to It.

End of the World?

Swami Chinmayananda in France. 1983

Further reading:

Art of man-making by Swami Chinmayananda
Self–Unfoldment, for BMI chart explanation by Swami Chinmayananda
Vivekchoodamani: verse 17, commentary by Swami Chinmayananda
Mandukya Karika: Chapter I
Katha Upanishad: Chapter II verse 16, commentary by Swami Chinmayananda
Ik Omkar commentary by Swami Swaroopananda, also audio cassette.

Vasanas

Swami Chinmayananda in Chessiers-Villars, Switzerland. 1984.

Vasanas at the intellectual level express themselves as desires,
at the mental level as agitations, and at the body level as actions.

Innate Psychological Tendencies

The mind is made up of soft matter as it were. As each thought passes through it, an impression is left on the mind-stuff like a scratch, and when similar thoughts are repeated it deepens into a canal. Every subsequent thought wave has got a tendency to flow though that ready made thought canal. Thus, if the impression or the canal made is of good thought-waves, then a good character is maintained, and strengthened by the subsequent thought waves flowing irresistibly in that direction.

When an action is undertaken with egocentric desires – the 'I' and 'I want' attitudes – that action leaves its impressions as *vasanas.* Thus when a person drinks with an attitude of 'I am enjoying', 'I want to have it', you find him growing into a habit of drinking. A person who takes brandy for six weeks as a medicine, does not develop that habit, if the intention is to cure an illness.

A criminal mind becomes a professional murderer with each added man-slaughter; while an army officer, though he has killed many, never becomes a murderer.

Vasanas, or **psychological tendencies, are the store house of our suppressions and repressions**. To exhaust this *vasana* burden, the secret lies in *Karma Yoga*. Karma Yoga is an attitude in action, in which one fixes the vision high. An army officer's vision is for the nation, and in a spirit of self-surrender and dedication, the mind gets purified and the *vasanas* get automatically exhausted.

Karma Yoga, the path of action, is a highly scientific way-of-life, which all of us can easily adopt once we have understood its entire implications. The world of objects and beings remaining the same, every one us, in whatever condition we may be at present, can learn to slowly grow to unbelievable heights, gathering to ourselves a new stature, undreamt of by anyone around us at any time.

For further reading: Kena Upanishad: Introduction
Bhagawad Geeta Chapter III
Vivekchoodamani – Commentary by Swami Chinmayananda

Telephone Vedanta

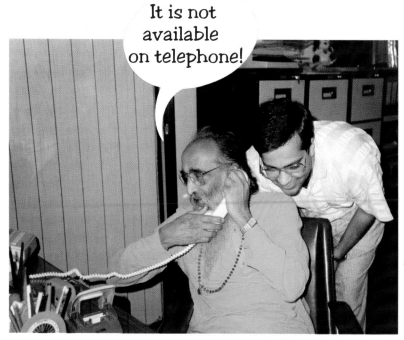

Swami Chinmayananda at Taipei, Taiwan. 1987.

Self Knowledge cannot be imparted over the telephone .....
Self Realization is not like going to a shopping centre and collecting it
in a shopping bag, throwing it in the back seat and driving away.
It is much deeper than that.

Crash Course in Spirituality

These days, unfortunately, we find seekers who think nothing about calling over the phone to enquire from the teacher at the other end of the city about the goal of life, the path, means, and so on. Such telephone tuition is not possible in spirituality. The seeker of spiritual life is asked to approach the master in an attitude of reverence and surrender. Then alone can the teacher acquaint the disciple with the knowledge of the Self.

"To know" in Vedanta means "to realize the Self". It is not an intellectual grasp, nor is it a result of mere study and reflection. Perfection will not be attained unless a person is ready to live the noble values of life, and through diligent and constant meditation - slowly and steadily - raise his purified mind and intellect to a higher realm of awareness and all-pervading consciousness.

Inspired flashes of wisdom are possible in rare moments of life such as during study, or when listening to a master. At such moments, an individual gets a glimmer of the higher possibility of the greater consciousness. But rare indeed is the man who is completely established in his identity with the higher. Such a rare one sits ever merged in the Self, extremely relaxed and completely happy as a result of the infinite merits acquired in the many, many lives in the past. When he thus lives established in his divine Self, he is the most revered one on the surface of the earth.

Further reading: Mananam: Self Discovery page 71

U Turn!

Swami Chinmayananda at the St. Louis crystal factory in France 1983. Photograph by Kamal Bhavnani

U Turn!

"You can" is the confident assurance given by all masters to everyone who has approached them for guidance.

You change, and the world around you will change!

Change the texture of your thoughts and your life will change.

Without changing the old, the new dimensions of life and living cannot be achieved. **You have to give up imitating the false values of others around you.** Stop living blindly a stamped blue-print of life supplied by the fashions of the times, or by the sensuous men who seek their fulfillment in a fruitless life of mere sense indulgences.

Just living the routine life of any unintelligent imitation of others in society is the surest way to plunge into a passionate life of sensuality. All psychological cowards, often unconsciously live this life of escapism. This sense of 'escapism' is detrimental to any great achievement.

The thick coating of memories and desires in one's personality takes away one's moral fire. In spite of man's self-glorification and social status, he is indeed a coward to himself with no confidence in his own goodness.

If you compromise due to lack of courage, you must have the heroism to suffer for it.

Audio Cassettes:
You change! by Swami Chinmayananda
How to Master the Mind by Swami Tejomayananda
The Science of Life Management by Swami Swaroopananda

Prescription from the Guru!

Read 2 stanzas of the Bhagawad Geeta 3 times a day for 3 months. If symptoms persist, repeat the dose.

The Bhagawad Geeta - not outdated!

The Pandava prince represents the confused man of the world – the disillusioned youth of all times. The case history of Arjuna is recorded with scientific precision in the opening chapter of the Bhagawad Geeta.

To get ourselves over-ridden by life's circumstances is to ensure disastrous failures on all occasions. Only a weakling, who allows himself to be overpowered by circumstances, can be victimized by the outer happenings. In his neurotic condition, Arjuna had become a slave to the outer challenges.

The youth often find their hopes shattered, their visions belied, their ambitions thwarted. The negative forces around them seem to gather more strength at every moment, and naturally, a sense of disillusionment verging on the point of hysteria and despondency overwhelms the youth. Their minds drooping in despondency, physically they come to live an unholy and unnatural life of excesses and shameless corruption, justifying everything they do in a mad sequence of noisy logic. This we find today among the youth all over the world.

Be it an individual or a society, in a community or a nation, **religion and philosophy will be in demand only when the heart has come to experience the Arjuna-grief.**

Krishna's psychological treatment for the Pandava prince constitutes the main theme of the Bhagawad Geeta.

The Geeta-educated man learns to recognize a rhythm, to see a **beauty,** to hear a **melody** in the ordinary day-to-day life — a life which was till then but a mad death-dance of appearances and disappearances of things and beings.

Further reading: The Holy Geeta – commentary by Swami Chinmayananda
                    Art of Man Making by Swami Chinmayananda

49 Video Cassettes of the discourses by Swami Chinmayananda, on the entire 18 chapters of the Bhagawad Geeta, recorded in Piercy, California, U.S.A.

Adhikaries

Swami Chinmayananda in Vienna, Austria. 1982.

The Fit Ones

One who feels charmed by the call of Vedanta, who can appreciate its arguments, who feels a sympathetic understanding of the ideal indicated, is indeed at the fag end of his transmigrations, the product of an entire evolutionary past. If he makes use of his present chance with diligent and careful application, success is guaranteed to him by Vedanta. **This is a call to man to throw off his lethargy, his dejections, his sentiments of self-pity and to wake up to face life,** and through understanding, to grow fast to reach the goal, here and now.

All of us, educated in modern colleges, who have a capacity to think for ourselves, have an awakened intellect, a heart of abiding emotions, a balanced character and an adventurous spirit to live the higher values of life – are all fit *adhikarins* to enter the spiritual kingdom. **Every intelligent person of culture and mental purity has a right to the great heritage of our *Rishis*.**

Vedanta contains the cream of all human experiences. The declarations of the *Rishis* have been formulated after close observations of the outer and inner lives of man - not at a given period of history, but through generations of teachers and disciples. Such a great wealth of knowledge cannot be the personal property of either an individual or a community or a nation. Vedanta, the science of life, is the common wealth of man, and every full grown man, who has started asking questions upon the logic of creation, the goal of life, the state of perfection, etc., has a right of free access to it, irrespective of his caste, creed or nationality, age or stage in life.

Further reading: Vivekchoodamani commentary by Swami Chinmayananda
                    Isavasya Upanishad: Introduction by Swami Chinmayananda

The Theory of Cause and Effect

Swami Chinmayananda in Sidhbari, India. 1985.

The past is the future modified in the present.
What you meet in life is *prarabdha;*
how you meet it is *purushartha.*

The Law of Karma

The Law of Karma is based on the theory of cause and effect, but has often been misunderstood as the fatalistic law of destiny.

Upon enquiry, we are driven to the conclusion that we are the different effects arising from different causes. Each of our actions from the past has its own reaction and each of us must have a treasure house of the entire past actions. So, **what we call destiny is the result of our past actions.**

The action of today becomes the destiny of tomorrow. Every action has its own reaction. Certain actions give their reaction immediately, while others provide their reaction after an interval. At each moment of our life, we are not only living the fruits of past actions, but also creating those of tomorrow. From the seed, the tree comes. The seed is the cause and the tree is the effect. The past causes the present and the present causes the future.

This law is indeed an omnipotent power that rules, governs over, controls and directs all life everywhere at all time. Thought by thought, new channels can be created: flowering seeds sewn, weeds plucked out and in time, the jungle in our mind can be rendered into a fragrant garden. By self-effort, everything is possible. Man can, with the right understanding, guide destiny.

Life has two movements: forward and lateral. This is like the movement of a car on the road. The petrol will merely push the car forward. The lateral movements are controlled by the driver. This forward dash in space is called destiny; and the lateral movement is called self effort. If the driver is drunk, the forward movement shall reach the gutters on the side in a tragic crash. But if the driver be intelligent, careful at every yard of the vehicle's movement, he can take us to our destination safely.

Man has been preparing bit by bit, a blue print of his life by his choice of action. The edifice of external environment and inner impulses in which he finds himself is of his own making, while his present choice is within the limitations of that edifice. *What* you meet in life is ***prarabdha***, destiny; *how* you meet it is ***purushartha***, self-effort.

continued...

Fair Share!

All our activities are called *karma*. **Karma is of three types**.
It is classified with reference to the past, present and future.

The total impressions gained by an individual through his
activities and thoughts accumulated at the unconscious level
of the mind are called *sanchita* – acquired. The large number
of *vasanas* within are all **sanchita karma.**

Of them, a few become fructified (*phalon-mukta*) and surge
forth to express. Because of such *vasanas,* we express
ourselves the way we do. These are called **prarabdha karma**,
that which has started yielding fruit.

There are yet other *vasanas* which are awaiting maturity.
They are yet to become effective. Such *vasanas* are called
agami.

The *sanchita* and the *agami*, both are destroyed at the moment
of Self-Realization. But this body being *prarabdha*, that which
is the result of past actions which have already started yielding
fruit, has to continue existing till it exhausts the momentum
with which it was born.

The body is the arrow which has already started from the
mother's womb and has been aimed at the tomb. From the
womb to the tomb is its journey. In that flight, having started
its career, nobody can stop it.

Further reading:
Kena Upanishad: Introduction, Law of Karma.
On Wings and Wheels by Swami Chinmayananda: Question on Free Will – Page 23
Vivekchoodamani verse 448 onwards

Karma

Reincarnation

Reincarnation is not a belief, but an assumption put forward based on the law of cause and effect. Religion must be supported by a philosophy that logically explains what we see and experience around us, and its relationship to the higher reality. How else would you explain the differences and the injustices that you see in the world? **Why is one man born a king and another a beggar?** When the disparities in life do not arise from any visible cause, they must be the effect of some invisible past cause or causes.

Although you do not remember all the thoughts and experiences you had in the last birth, the subtle impressions they left are still with us. They provide the motivation or a driving force for another manifestation, another birth as a human. It is not by accident that you are what you are and I am what I am. We are all products of our past. The *Law of Karma* is based upon the final conclusion that this life is not an end in itself, but is just one of the little incidents in the eternal existence in each one of us.

People do not come from nowhere, and at their death do not become mere non-existent nothingness. Correct philosophical thinking guides man's intellect to the apprehension of a continuity from the past – through the present – to the endless future. The spirit remaining the same, it gets seemingly conditioned by different body-equipments, and comes to live through its self-ordained environments.

It is this conclusion of the Hindu philosophers that has given them the most satisfactory *Theory of Reincarnation.* The most powerful opponents of this idea do not seem to have studiously followed their own Scriptures. Christ himself has, if not directly, at least indirectly, proclaimed this doctrine when he told his disciples: "John, the Baptist, was Elijah". Origin, the most learned of the Christian fathers, has clearly declared: "Every man received a body for himself according to his deserts in former lives."

continued......

Born Lucky!

There was no great thinker in the past who had not, or any in the present who has not accepted, expressly or tacitly, these logical conclusions about the doctrine of reincarnation. Buddha constantly made references to his previous births. Virgil and Ovid regarded the doctrine as perfectly self-evident. Josephus observed that the belief in reincarnation was widely accepted among the Jews of his age. Solomon's Book of Wisdom says: "To be born in sound body with sound limbs is a reward of the virtues of the past lives."

And who does not remember the famous saying of the learned son of Islam who declared: "I died out of the stone and became a plant; I died out of the plant and became an animal; I died out of the animal and became a man. Why then do I fear to die? When did I grow less by dying? I shall die out of man and shall become an angel!"

In later times, this most intelligent philosophical belief has been accepted as a doctrine by the German philosophers Goethe, Fichte, Schelling and Lessing. Among the recent philosophers, Hume, Spencer, Max Mueller, have all recognised this doctrine as incontrovertible. Among the poets of the West also, we find many burnished intellects soaring into the cloudless sky of imagination, and within their poetic flights, they too have intuitively felt the sanction behind this immortal doctrine – Browning, Rossetti, Tennyson and Wordsworth - to mention but a few names.

The *Reincarnation Theory* is not a mere dream of the philosophers, and the day is not far off when, with the fast developing science of psychology, the West will come to rewrite its Scripture under the sheer weight of observed phenomena. **An uncompromising intellectual quest for understanding life cannot satisfy itself, if it is thwarted at every corner by "observed irregularities."**

Further reading: Commentary on The Holy Geeta by Swami Chinmayananda, Chapter II verse 12.

Beginningless!

Concept of time

'anaadi' ———————— ●————— ●————— ●
Beginningless | unit of time

Third experience
(2nd unit of time= second
second)

first experience
before time
was created

second experience
and the first unit
of time is created
(first second)
(i.e. concept of time)

requires the existence of
  1) experiencer, the subject
  2) the object of experience
  3) and the relationship between the two

The cause for above three is
ignorance of one's true Self.

When did Creation Start?

In Vedanta we do not believe that creation started at any known point in time. This would be illogical and unacceptable to any awakened thinker.

Time can express itself only in a mind that experiences. In deep sleep there is no concept of time. Time cannot be perceived and experienced unless there is a field of objects – the world. If we say that creation started, at let us say, "21st September" (creation hour!), 21st September can have any sense or meaning, only with reference to 20th September (when creation was not!). This would be absurd, as time itself is a created perishable concept. To avoid these logical contradictions, the only way we can say when creation started would be 0 second, 0 minute, 0 date, 0 week, 0 month, 0 year. **Time is the space between two experiences. So the *first* unit of time gets created only with the *second* experience, which means that creation has already come to pass (in the first experience).** The concept of time was non-existent in the first experience. This idea is more beautifully and scientifically put when we say "The creation is beginningless", *anadi,* before time. Since it is beginningless, it is absurd to think of the first creation.

According to Vedanta, there is no creation in the sense of something having come out of nothing. God is himself both the material and the efficient cause of the universe. There was no first cycle. Time is infinite. If you give a beginning to time, the whole concept of time will be destroyed.

Why did God create the Universe?

Such questions are logical absurdities! Reason exists in nature. Beyond nature it has no existence. God is omnipotent, hence to ask **why he did this or that is to limit him**; for it implies that he must have had a purpose in creating the universe. **If he had a purpose, it must be a means to an end,** and this would mean that he could not have the end without the means. Then questions, "why and wherefore", can only be asked of something that depends upon something else.The perfection of God is unlike any finite perfection. **It is perfection of the infinite and this includes all finite possibilities.** At least, we may conceive of the infinite artist in the joy of his artistry, producing forever new forms; the infinite lover in the joy of his being, forever creating new objects out of his love. The extollation of the infinite can have no limits.

Further reading: Aitareya Upanishad:Introduction page16-18 and text page 33 onwards.
Prasna Upanishad commentary by Swami Chinmayananda,verse 4.
The Mystery of Creation:Vedantic explanation of creation pages 8–22

"Avatar"

Swami Chinmayananda in Sidhbari, India. 1990. Drawing on top by Swami Chinmayananda.

Incarnations of the Lord

The word *avatar* means *fallen*. The Infinite fallen from its supreme state into an apparent state of finitude and sorrow is *avatar*. The entire universe is an expression of the infinite reality, but **an *avatar* is ever conscious of his own infinite nature.**

The Supreme, on account of his unquestioned freedom, by his own perfectly free will, takes upon himself the matter envelopments and manifests himself in a particular embodiment in the world, for serving the deluded generation of the time. To the Lord, this "ignorance" is a pose assumed, not a fact lived. ***Avatars* are answers to the silent prayers of the good**, when they too tend to become bad at the onslaught of the evil-minded.

In the *avatars,* we watch a greater effulgence of the divine consciousness constantly expressed, and they embody forth whenever there is an excessive decline of *dharma,* righteousness, and the rise of *adharma*, unrighteousness, in the world.

Though the Lord is unborn and changeless in his nature, and ever a Lord of matter, yet, keeping his *maya*, power of delusion, perfectly under his own control, **he comes into the world through his own free will, fully conscious of his own divine status and unchallenged prerogative.**

He does not come into being as others do, compelled by his past *karma,* to live in this world under the thralldom of nature. He is not bound by his mental temperaments, but he is ever free from the mischief of his own *maya*.

Whenever there is a decline of *dharma* (righteousness, the law of being) and when the majority of people do not obey this great truth, there being a conquest of this world by a herd of bi-peds — **then in all such dark periods of history, the infinite Lord wears the matter-apparel, the garb of the finite**, and appears on the scene of activity, like the owner of an estate, who now and then puts on his gum boots to inspect and re-organize his estate.

continued…

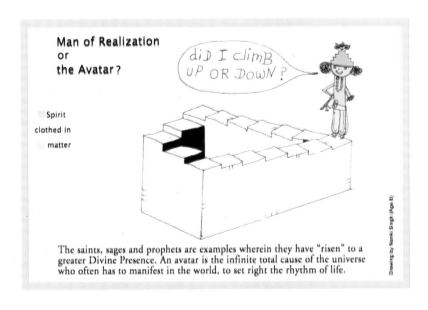

Man of Realization
or
the Avatar?

did I climb UP OR DOWN?

Spirit
clothed in
matter

The saints, sages and prophets are examples wherein they have "risen" to a greater Divine Presence. An avatar is the infinite total cause of the universe who often has to manifest in the world, to set right the rhythm of life.

Drawing by Namiki Singh (Age 8)

Incarnations **"descend"**, as it were, from the unmanifest Supreme Essence into the world of matter, fully conscious of their divine nature. Saints and sages **"ascend"** to realize their divinity, by detaching their identification with their matter vestures.

Similarly, the Supreme, who is the substratum for the pluralistic world, puts on the body-gown and, as it were, walks into the dusty atmosphere of the immoral life of mankind, for the purpose of re-organizing and conducting a thorough spring cleaning of the bosom of man. He reserves for himself, the divine freedom to be in the body, and yet not of it. This he does for the protection of the good and for the destruction of the wicked (wrong tendencies).

It is important to understand that for those who cannot accept the *saguna,* the concept of the Lord having an embodiment, but are practising sincerely and whole heartedly, seeking the truth without form, *nirguna*, the goal is equally available to them.

The sages, saints and prophets are different from incarnations, in that they are born as mortals, and through study and meditation rise higher to experience the opening up of a fuller consciousness. They are all examples wherein we find a greater divine presence.

The individual person's innate desires are his own personal debt. The total of everyone's innate desires is the national debt. Spiritual teachers function only at this total level. They come in response to the cry of people for an escape from their suffering and for an understanding of the meaning of life. The teacher comes to guide them. When they point in the direction of the bazaar, one must get up and go. If he sits there and hangs on to his finger, he will never experience the joys of the bazaar. When the teacher directs him, he cannot sit there hanging on to his words. Everyone has got to go in that direction for himself; no *guru* can do it for him.

When one puts sugar in one's coffee, one must stir it in or the coffee will still be bitter. The teacher puts spiritual ideas into one's mind but to get the sweetness, one must stir them with the process of his own independent reflection, away from the support of all props.

Further reading: The Holy Geeta, Chapter IV verses 4 – 5.
                     Art of Man-Making by Swami Chinmayananda
Audio Cassettes: Krishna Avatar by Swami Chinmayananda
                     Adi Sankara by Swami Chinmayananda
CDs. Video & Audio Cassettes:
                     Shrimad Bhagawat by Swami Tejomayananda
                     Ram Charit Manas by Swami Tejomayananda

Man of God Realization

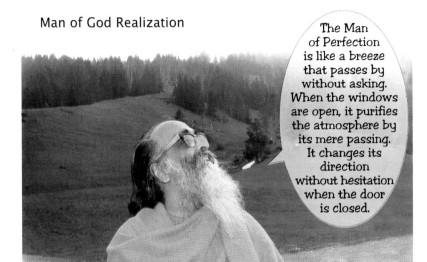

The Man of Perfection is like a breeze that passes by without asking. When the windows are open, it purifies the atmosphere by its mere passing. It changes its direction without hesitation when the door is closed.

Swami Chinmayananda near Villars, Switzerland, 1984.

Man of God Realization

Do not expect a man of perfection and God realization to fall in line with one whom you have known. We see saints and sages in all conditions; Janaka as a king, Jata Bharata as a lunatic, Dattatreya as a wandering man with no sense of the world outside – some naked, some singing and some meditating, some talking and some in *mauna*, some exhibiting powers and others proving themselves as useless as any idiot. So don't try to estimate a great spiritual teacher with reference to the past patterns known to you. **In their external behaviour etc., they are all a law unto themselves.** But, watch their face – is there an extra glow? Are they equanimous in all conditions? Have they unbroken love, endless tolerance, limitless cheerfulness, patience and education? Are they kind and benign? Do they radiate warmth of the soul? Do they command silently the agitations in your hearts? Do you feel divinized, enlightened, encouraged and comforted in their presence? Then, they are the real master - minds merged in God consciousness.

Men of achievement are very few indeed. **It is these people who give a fillip to the general cultural beauty of society and uplift the entire generation to a higher standard of life, a higher dignity of morality, a greater virtue in living.** Such mighty men are called saints and seers, prophets or incarnations of great virtues and values. They live an ideal life, inspiring others even after their death. The fragrance of their thought, and the might and glory of their ideals, gather a new momentum as the years pass by. Christ died two thousand years ago, and yet we find that his glory becomes more and more compelling as time passes.

One may ask the man of achievement: "What is it that you want in the world; why are you working? O Buddha, why did you work; O Christ, why did you work; O Mohammed, why did you move from place to place, preaching against many odds?" A man of achievement works in the world not for profit, nor for success or recognition, but from a feeling of self-fulfillment that he did the best he could. He does not care whether others recognize him or not. He is a master of circumstances, a ruler of his own generation.
– Thus, the sage walks the earth in the strides of a god!

Coffee! Coffee!!

Swami Chinmayananda in New Delhi, India. 1989.

Audio Cassette: Chief Executive Officer(CEO)by Swami Swaroopananda

Earn - Enjoy - Save

There is no harm if things and beings are around us, but mentally we should not hug them with a sense of ownership. Let a man of intelligence *earn* as much as he can, distribute according to his abilities, and *enjoy* as much as is his desserts – popularity, affection, consideration and even reverence from others. But let him not misunderstand this to be the very goal of life. At the same time, let him also earn inner peace and self-sufficiency and let him *save* the inner peace and tranquility, totally independent of all the clamouring crowd around him, ever trying to fatten his vanities and feed, at all times, his conceit! **The real achievement is to be gained in one's own personal inner contemplation, long before the world comes to reject him.**

The power to *earn* and *save* should include all powers, spiritual and secular, everywhere, at all levels in the society: the capacity of a scientist, of the politician, of an artist, of a teacher, of a speaker, of a manufacturer and so on.

The Vedantic concept of renunciation has nothing to do with 'have' or 'have not' in a physical sense; it means an *attitude* of non-attachment. The classical example in our ancient lore is that of Emperor Janak, living in the luxury of a palace, but still considered such a saint and sage, that great aspirants went to him for guidance.

Rich and Famous!

Matter? Never Mind!
Mind? Doesn't Matter!

Swami Chinmayananda in London, U.K. and child in Nairobi, Kenya in 1986. Double exposure photograph!

The dreamer is in fact the waker, but he spreads an entire world of OET (objects, emotions and thoughts) around him.

Spirit and Matter

Matter is the mental projection in a solidified form. **Matter has no existence of its own, for there is no such matter found in modern science which can be known as *prima particle* or matter as such.** Everything seems to be known through its characteristics i.e. colour, form, smell, etc. The universe is defined in terms of our sensation which is nothing but our mental conceptions and feelings.

Sensation does not depend on matter. **Dreams are dreamt without matter.** In dreams we have a sensation, as real as in this world, without the existence of external things! We say the dream world is unreal because it disappears during our waking. The waking world also disappears in the dream.

This world can be defined only on the basis of our mental condition, not on the basis of external things.

Feelings are the last atoms of the external world. Feeling belongs to the feeler, and the feeler is this "I", the Self. To experience the Self is to know the real relationship between the external and internal world. The whole world is nothing but the Self.

"As we think, so we become." All through life, when an individual is trying to transcend the body, mind and intellect - the world of matter - by living the higher life of purity, he comes to experience the glory of the spirit.

Further reading: Prasna Upanishad commentary by Swami Chinmayananda:
verses 5 to 16
Vedanta through Letters Part I, page 108, (Old Edition)
Bhagawad Geeta chapter XIII
Bhagawad Geeta chapter XV verses 7,8,9

Love?

Fall in love is when your peace of mind is gone and your abilities distracted.

Rise in love is devotion to any ideal, profession, art, science or person that makes you integrated and creative.

Devotion gives you more intellectual capacities, abilities improve. You become dynamic-a person to be reckoned with.

Swami Chinmayananda in Mumbai, India 1975.

The human mind always runs in the direction of his love. The object of love reflects his *vasanas*, his tendencies.

Types of Love

No activity in human life is taken up with so much sincerity and elaborate preparation as is man's search for the joy of love, and yet, no enterprise of man fails so constantly, with such regularity, as his quest for love. He helplessly waits to receive love, and yet everyone is always disappointed.

In a nutshell, **the love that leaves us with agitation in our mind is lower love,** and the love that leaves us with profound peace and joy is higher. **In true love, every action and sacrifice you make towards the object of your love reduces your egocentric desires and calms the agitation in your mind**. When love is directed towards a nobler or higher object or person than yourself, it is called *prema.* And when it is towards a lower object, it is called *sneha.* Higher love alone can help us come out of our sense of incompleteness and alienation.

The **lower type of love** called *sneha* **is an escape from a person's sense of loneliness.** Without this protection the person feels lonely, isolated and helpless. Such people demand love, they need to receive it – they cannot give love. **Such an individual depends entirely upon other objects and beings for his existence: his home, work, money, friends and relations. With these he makes a prison for himself and ever willingly suffers in it.** This refers to both past-passive and aggressive type of *sneha.* They are both unconsciously seeking freedom from their sense of loneliness.

The higher kind of love is called *prema*. Here, love is **dynamic**. The lover is not waiting to be loved by others. He is not a beggar of love. His dynamic love floods forth from its heart and in its irresistible onward dash, it breaks all walls around others, storms into their hearts and therein seeks and discovers a blissful fusion of oneness. In this dynamic love, **the lover ennobles the beloved and at the same time retains his own individuality.** In such a blessed love-relationship the two become one, and still neither dominates the other, nor is anyone rendered a victim of the other. In dynamic love, it is a willful "dashing on" to love, rather than

Not so easy!

DISC DIVISION
WHAT IF EVERYONE WAS LIKE YOU SWAMIJI
VICE-CHAIRMAN
WHAT IF EVERYBODY TOOK 'SANYASA' AND RAN AWAY FROM SOCIETY? HUH? WHAT THEN?
WHAT IF EVERYONE IN THE WHOLE WORLD SUDDENLY DECIDED TO RUN AWAY FROM SOCIETY?
TRY!

an unconscious accidental "falling into" love. It is a consistent passion to give, not a meek persistent hope to receive. True loving is not a passive taking, but a dynamic giving.

This idea of giving is often dreaded and misunderstood as a giving up of something – a painful renouncing – a state of being deprived of everything pleasant and sweet. But actually, it is a *giving up of all the anxiety* to enjoy the fruits of actions.

Love, when it is true and unconditional, is its own reward. Very few realize it, none dare to live it. **Some of us love only if we are loved in return.** That is, we give love in payment for the love received. This is a commercial attitude, a shopkeeper's mentality. To give love is freedom; to demand love is pure slavery.

If you want others to love you, be lovable. Love cannot be lust. In lust, there is abject dependence upon the physical object. In lust, there is a subordination of one's personality to the enchantment of the object; **while in love, the personality of the lover is tuned to the personality of the beloved.** Love brings an expansion of being, while lust ends in an existence loaded with darkness and exhausting fatigue. Love is the victory of the spirit, lust is the cry of the base flesh and low mind. **Love lives the joy; lust only seeks it.**

Very few are rich in love. How can they love, who have none in themselves? **Love transforms work into inspiration with efficiency as its result.**

Love is the heart of religions, the theme of all classical works of art and literature, the song of all devotees. Scientists know only what love does – not what love is. Love can indeed empty our asylums, perhaps all our prisons, maybe all our hospitals. People suffer in life due to lack of love. Love is to human hearts what the sun is to flowers!

Further reading:
"I love you" letters by Swami Chinmayananda
On Wings and Wheels by Swami Chinmayananda: the question on Intense Love
Mananam: Source of Inspiration, chapter on Types of Love – page 16
Narada Bhakti Sutra – Aphorisms on Love, commentary by Swami Chinmayananda
Mananam: The Path of Love, chapter on Love in Action
CD & Cassette: Managing love and relationships by Swami Swaroopananda

Broken heart?

Don't worry! The heart is the only instrument that is guaranteed for life!

Swami Chinmayananda for a heart check up at a hospital in New Jersey, U.S.A. 1985.

I inaugurated the outpatients' ward of the hospital that day. Today, I inaugurate the inpatients' ward!

How to mend a Broken Heart

When, having procured an object-of-desire, the object decays in the embrace of the mind, the sorrow suffered by the mind is called **grief.** When an obstacle comes between the mind and the object of desire, then the emotion that arises to disturb the mind is called **anger.**

Many tragedies reach all of us. Nothing is a tragedy to those who know how to contact them rightly. **Be an intelligent witness of every happening within and without.** Let all around you, including your body, enjoy and live through what is their *prarabdha* (the results of their past actions). Keep on gazing at what is happening all around you – quite an interested witness, but not an attached one. Life is a huge *tamasha*, joke; there can be no occasion to feel melancholy, wounded, crushed, disappointed or thwarted.

Grief and dejection are the price that delusion demands from its victim. To rediscover ourselves to be really something higher than our own ego, is to end all the sorrows that have come to us through our false identifications. **When human beings** in their freedom to act and think **have followed wrong tendencies** for a long time, they must be **helped to rediscover their mental purity and right discrimination.** They come to lose their mental equipoise and in their inner confusion and sensuous excesses, they sink to live at the level of animals. At such moments, they need the discipline of sorrow, the pangs of punishment, the agony of watching the total disaster of their false world of glory. Such painful experiences alone can drive home to them the folly of their empty values, the tragedy of their false purposes, the painful end of their panting excesses. **Pain is the Lord's kindest means to wake us up the quickest.**

The Lord does not judge or forgive; yet when a student realizes the folly of his past hopes and expectations and ardently expresses his wish to come out of their strangulating grip, the poignancy of his own powerful thought *sankalpas* blesses him. The negative *vasanas*, product of his past actions undertaken in ignorance, die away

continued.....

Shaky Ground!

Swami Chinmayananda coming down the steps of Jagadeeshwara Temple, Powai, Mumbai. 1984.

How can you depend upon that which is itself shaky and subject to change? The world of objects, emotions and thoughts is undergoing constant change.

automatically. **The individual needs to follow a system of right values, when there is no clear conviction of the existence of a larger goal in life.**

You will notice that as time passes, the pain of the separation will not be as strong as on the day of the happening. Why is it so? Because it was painful, you did not think of it often. **The less one thinks of a thing, the less one gets attached to it**. The opposite is also equally true: the more you think of a thing the more you get attached to it.

With all its sham drudgery and broken dreams, it is still a beautiful world. Be careful. Strive to be happy.

Pray. Prayer has a strength, unbelievable indeed, until we start praying. During prayer, we dive, as it were, into ourselves, and diving deep, come out of the depth with precious pearls of energy, strength and vitality, to the surface of our own personality.

There is nothing in life that can ever happen which is that much serious as to deserve our tears. Never brood over things that have happened or worry over things yet to happen. Live in the present intelligently. Face life with a tranquil heart.

Don't underwrite away your whole life – **hanging down all the time on a thin thread of some grace of love given or shown to you by somebody.** Be a grown-up giant of spiritual strength that you can give love to the whole world and bathe the world in it.

LET GO — let it go....... where it goes!

Further reading: Art of Man Making by Swami Chinmayananda

Attachment – a knot

Sigh! ....
I wish I had
a doll.

All sorrows are a
result of our wrong
relationship with the objects
of the world outside.

You want
me to change
my entire mental
attitude, when
a 'doll' could
solve the
problem?

(People go to mahatmas and ask for trivial things or to solve their
domestic problems, when they could ask for the complete solution
to life's problems.)

Swami Chinmayananda at Santa Cruz University Camp, California, U.S.A. 1982.

The knots of the heart are; *avidya*, ignorance; *kama*, desire
and *karma*, action. When a human being, during his lifetime,
breaks asunder these bonds, he, in fact, ends his ignorance.
Ignorance can be ended only with knowledge.

Further reading:
The Holy Geeta, Chapter II commentary by Swami Chinmayananda

The Slippery Fall

When a thought-flow towards a given object or being becomes continuous, it becomes **attachment**. All our attachments to the world are forged with our own continuous thoughts. When this attachment increases in its force of flow, it begets the feeling of **longing** (or desire) to possess the object of attachment. When that desire is thwarted, the very desire-thoughts, so disappointed and frustrated, putrify to give out the foul stink of **anger.**

The anger gathers in dark chunks, which roll themselves into a dreary shroud to cloud reason, thus entering into a state of sheer **delusion**, meaning, seeing things that are not. When you get really angry with me, you start seeing me as a horned devil, morally abhorrent, ethically fallen, devilishly plotting your destruction. The angry man has his own hallucinations and self-deluding dreams; he cannot see things as they are. In his upset mind, his perceptions become false, his estimates vague, his judgments wrong, and naturally his actions wild and uncontrolled.

From this delusion of mind froths up **loss of memory.** Every experience, subjective and objective, leaves its record in us as a memory. The total memory of our direct and indirect experiences together becomes our present wisdom. One is a great doctor, another a mighty scientist, another a brilliant scholar but all these are memories of the individuals. Memory, here, means knowledge and wisdom of the individual gained from his experiences. When we get angry, our actions are not guided by our knowledge. Even against our own father or teacher we would readily lift our hand. Wisdom, the total accumulated experiences in us, preserved as memories, gets lost. When wisdom is lost, the individual's **power of discrimination**, which is his intellect, also **gets lost**.

Man's superiority over the animals is his discriminative power. When this does not function, such a man falls low and he **perishes.** Thus, what starts as a simple stream of idle sensuous thoughts can make man lose everything. Remember, **the fall down the ladder of devolution to utter disaster is caused by a slip in self-control**. When wrong thoughts were buzzing through us, we were not alert enough to control their traffic.

The Yoga of 'Attachment–Detachment'

Swami Chinmayananda in Nairobi, Kenya. 1985.

Nature abhors vacuum.
When you are trying to detach, hold on to something else, something
nobler–until you 'unhang' yourself from all your 'hangups'!

Divorce from Sorrow

The more one thinks of a thing, the more one gets attached to it - and the less one thinks of it, the less one gets attached to it.

Thoughts running continuously towards a particular object can create attachment to it. **When the thought flow is reduced, the attachment is diminished.**

The same principle is adopted by *japa* and *kirtan. Japa* (repetition of the Lord's name) is the training of the mind in fixing itself to a single line of thinking. ***Japa*, if properly done, can bring about a sustained single pointedness more efficiently, than all the hasty methods of meditation.**

People who have distinguished themselves in different vocations, owe their successes to single pointed efforts with a tenacity of purpose, while failures in life are marked by want of concentration of the mind.

A common phenomenon which demonstrates the power of concentration is **the effect of the sun's rays** on an object. The rays of the sun have no perceptible effect upon the object, but **when they are converged to a single point**, with the aid of a powerful convex lens, the concentration at the point can ignite the object.

Japa should not be over practised. Start with a *mala, (*108 beads) of *japa* a day, repeat fervently your chosen *mantra* of the Lord.

Further reading:
Self-Unfoldment, chapter VIII on how to do *japa*: by Swami Chinmayananda
Art of Contemplation by Swami Chinmayananda
Meditation and Life by Swami Chinmayananda

Cassettes & CDs:
Gayatri Mantra by Swami Swaroopananda
Various bhajan and chanting cassettes by Swami Tejomayananda
and Swami Brahmananda
Geeta Chanting by Swami Brahmananda
Meditation - a new frontier by Swami Nikhilananda

Jogging for Health

Daily jog to Jagadeeshwara and walk back home to perform your duties.

The Power of Prayer

When problems regarding our rights and duties arise, challenging our security and comfort, when emotions spring up threateningly, when questions of our right relationship with the world of things and beings burst forth in tidal dimensions, when we face our self ruinous habits, world destroying ambitions, disturbing lusts, shattering selfishness, or benumbing sorrows, suddenly we realize that we are torn apart within. We have no answers to these inner problems, nor can we defend ourselves against them with all the artillery we have created, the scientific knowledge we have mounted or the incomparable era of prosperity and pleasure we have inaugurated. **The world has no remedy.**

The only instrument of defence is our mind. How are we to strengthen our fortress against the incessant onslaughts of the world of challenges around us? **This is done by turning our limited, conditioned mind to the total mind, the universal creative energy, God.** This higher mind is ever present everywhere, for all to partake of its infinite strength and endless solace.

The divine mind is ever ready to cooperate. Let us approach him through love. When our mind gets tuned to this **divine voltage,** we shall get **recharged,** and a mind so replenished from its inexhaustible splendour shall feel **rejuvenated, revived, fulfilled.**

This is true prayer. Pray, we must, but let it be revitalizing prayer – not a clamourous begging for gaining anything from him.

Let us, in prayerful meditation, realize what our real nature is, through the grace and strength supplied by the total mind, God, the Lord of our heart, the very Lord of the universe, Jagadeeswara, (*Jagat-Ishwara*).

Further reading: Mananam: The Power of Prayer
Various Bhajan Cassettes by Swami Tejomayananda and Swami Brahmananda
Adi Sankara Strotrams by Swami Brahmananda
Geeta Chanting by Swami Brahmananda
CD & Cassette: Get online with the Higher Power by Swami Swaroopananda

Swami Chinmayananda enroute Uttarkashi, India. 1985.

Stay Where You are Put

A spiritual seeker should not try to run away, in the very beginning into protection, but must court life and plunge into the centre of it and take life as it comes — good, bad or indifferent — and learn to balance himself in spite of all the imperfections in the circumstances. **A family, a brother, etc., are pieces set up around you to give a definite chosen experience, which alone will be conducive to your progress.** Take what life has to give you as the Lord's gift, *prasad.* Sorrows polish off the *vasanas* and tears are the brasso of the mind. **The eternal law provides each of us with a circumstance in life to enjoy or suffer strictly according to and in continuation of our past.** There are no accidents in the eternal law. Moment to moment, life is progressive, continual and logical.

What is to be avoided is not the world outside. Nowadays people say: "I am getting out of this place. This country is no good". When you run away from your country, do you think your country will improve, or are *you* going to improve? You will become a second grade citizen in another country. Have the honour, the self-respect to remain in the country and learn to live rightly. If we all start to live rightly, we will already have set the entire history on to the right channels and lifted the nation from the ruts to which it has fallen.

In the impulse of the moment, in a rising tide of disgust, at some specific failure, people often renounce in a hurry and run away from life. Such people, without exception, come to live in regret, suffering endless mental agony, arising out of their physical privations. The exhaustion and fatigue suffered by them in this subjective storm is the source of all worldly sorrows. This storm is in the mind, which they will carry wherever they go. What has to be changed is the mind, not the environment.

Let a person stay where he is stationed and placed in life which is all prescribed according to his psychological texture, and proceed according to the *karma*, work, that is allocated to him, the duties enjoined on him, according to his qualifications, his psychological nature, his *dharma.* **Doing his *dharma* he will be serving the higher cause.**

Further reading: On Wings and Wheels by Swami Chinmayananda Part I:
My station and its duties; conflicting standpoints; the goal; guidelines for judgement.

The Optimist and the Pessimist

Swami Chinmayananda in Melbourne, Australia.1987.

The Optimist and the Pessimist

One complains of bad times and a bad world. Half a glass full of milk is viewed differently by different people, according to their own emotional and intellectual stature.

A lame man on a wheel chair despairs at the sight of a healthy pair of legs walking past him. The man who can walk, envies the one on a scooter. The man on the scooter is jealous of the motor car owner and the motor car owner is worried about having to pay his income tax!

In a short sighted view, life presents in its circumscribed scope a look of tragedy - an occasion to sigh and weep. But in a far-sighted view, the very same life presents in its ampler scope an experience of comedy - an occasion to smile and laugh.

"**Change of Vision**" is the remedy recommended by all masters of truth who have gained the vision. Therefore keep smiling; all falls are a rise in the total.

By refusing to crave for objects which we do not have, we shall be conserving a lot of mental energy, which alone can give us peace and a capacity to act rightly in the world.

No true seeker has a right to be pessimistic; he should be ever consciously optimistic. Remember, behind each one of you there stand a million who can, at their best, grace only the lower rungs of the ladder of evolution. It is for the *man-animal* that the knowledge of the Self is rare and difficult. To those who are in the *man-man* state of evolution, the achievement of the goal of life is but a mere question of choice and a walk into the Temple of Perfection.

Be optimistic; and each of you may take it from Chinmaya: you are a fit *adhikarin,* and with a little self-effort you shall reach, in this very birth, the supreme success and Godly achievement. Never hesitate, never doubt. Strive and achieve.

Confidence

If we have the ability to surrender our selfish ego to a higher goal, then what others think of us will not matter. We surrender both our strength and weaknesses and draw our inspiration from that faith in the ideal, then the opinions of others cannot be an obstacle.

Confidence

In the grey areas of choice, why are you afraid? With whatever data is before you, go ahead and choose an action and carry it through. Even if the action chosen turns out to be a mistake, what does it matter? What do a few mistakes matter in one's long span of life? From the experience of the mistake learn to discriminate more keenly. Don't be afraid to act while doing the action. If you realize it is a mistake, don't become indecisive again and leave the action. Continue with the action and tell the mind "Now you suffer! You chose it, you suffer". And thereby learn to evaluate actions correctly and develop discrimination.

In order to face challenges, a lot of courage is necessary. Do not run away. **You must learn to face the situation.** The courage to face it comes only when the mind is strong and poised, only then can it rediscover its own efficiency, ability and beauty of performance – all of which ensure success in life.

How does this equipoise come about? It comes when an individual's mind is ignited by a larger vision, **when he comes to understand his importance in life, his nobility and the great contribution that he is expected to make during his lifetime.** Even though the situation outside seemed impossible earlier, he now develops the courage to face it. He realizes that he has been selected to do that particular job. He recognizes his own importance with the understanding that he is not a single solitary individual fighting against the world of multiplicity, but that he is one with the whole universe.

Further reading: On Wings and Wheels by Swami Chinmayananda, page 46
Vedanta in Action- page 15

Secret Recipe

Vitamins? Bah!
Vitamins cannot give
health by themselves.
It is our mental attitude
in life that is the real health.
Economise the mental energy.
And when that vigour is put
into work, a hundred times
more effective success can
be got out of it. This
is the Rishi secret.

Swami Chinmayananda in Port Blair, Andaman Islands, India.1991.

Good Health

At the physical level, weekly fasting is not advisable for a young person who is working all the week round with a severe routine. A lot of energy is needed for right living. Eat such foods as are easily digestible. It is not the gross calories that are needed, but the subtle energy born out of *sattvic* (pure) food. This is the fuel upon which our intellectual and spiritual life moves. You may not realize it now, but in the long run, when you want to 'raise' the engine and soar higher – then too late, alas – that you are in want of energy and strength.

We may look for biological causes for illnesses, but the root cause is mental. The body is a tool, wielded by the technician - the mind - behind it. The tool's performance depends upon the knowledge and ability of the technician. It is not our body, but the mind and intellect that is acting in us. When the mind is bright and alert, the actions are spectacular. But when the mind is exhausted, dissipated, moody or sorrowful, it reflects on the body. **Emotional and intellectual exhaustion decreases our physical capacity and brings about a sudden exhaustion – sleeplessness, high blood pressure and heart trouble.**

A typical industrialist may find that the bank is not releasing enough loans, or that the government is exerting pressure, or that labour is not co-operating. The cause of such anxieties is very subtle and you may not even be aware of it. All worries are due to the psychologically selfish notion that "I will work only for my family. I will have nothing to do with the world". Only if you can understand that you, industrialists especially (or other specialists), are a rare few, gifted by the Lord with the ability to produce wealth for society or nation, and you have been doing it successfully and will find a joy for doing it on a larger scale for others.

If the mind is happy, I am happy, if the mind is miserable, I am miserable. If my mind has negative thoughts, my actions are detrimental to myself and to other members of society; whereas the actions of a person with positive thoughts are a blessing to himself and to society. Why is the mind always in fear, hesitation, without dynamism or courage to take up a particular

All in the Mind!

Further reading:
On Wings and Wheels by Swami Chinmayananda Chapter III:
section on Vegetarianism.
Audio Cassettes:
Swasthya Yoga by Swami Tejomayananda
Journey in Health: Swami Swaroopananda

programme? What am I to do? Why am I wavering all the time?

What is it that orders the quality of thoughts? The texture and quality of thoughts are governed by the values that you uphold in life. **Every one of you has got a value for something – certain convictions that you have reached in your intellect as to what should be the direction of your life.** If your values are unhealthy, you can repair them with your intellect. Recognize your present negative values as dangerous and change the thought pattern to a higher ideal. The lower thoughts then change to a higher texture. This is how all great revolutions have come by. **The revolutionaries make people think in a direction. Unless the values of life are changed, the contours of our national life cannot change.** The inner wealth is the strength and vitality of your mind. Newton's law says that nothing can move without the *expenditure* of energy. When we worry, we waste a lot of mental energy, our wealth. This expenditure and exhaustion is evident on our face.

Suppose you have got the value of "I hate". You have got the freedom to hate anybody. **The person you hate sleeps well, eats well, but it is you who gets exhausted in hating.** But if you were to love that person even if he is harming you, it will not affect you, because certain values of life reduce the expenditure of energy and dissipation, making you efficiently face your own problems – economic, industrial, professional or domestic.

Revolutionalise your attitude to the world outside by bringing a total reorientation of your life. **Make it a success out of the failures of today; this is the highest art to work on yourself.** These values are love, tenderness, forgiveness, truthfulness and goodness. Knowing a thing and living up to it are totally different things. **To manage your life, the higher values are necessary, so that your reaction to the outside world does not dissipate your energy.**

If you are not going to face your challenges, you, the educated, will become extinct. **The illiterate's way of life is to imitate you.** You change your attitude to life and change the health and destiny of your nation.

To comfort a heart patient

Swami Chinmayananda in New Delhi.1980.

'Heart' represents the core of one's being,
the Inner Essence.

Service

The present is the product of the past. **The elder citizens' generation carved out for us our present, ill or well. We serve them in their old age when they are tired and fatigued, to sit back to rest and revive.** Duties and respect towards the elders should not only be at home, but towards all elder citizens around you.

A neglected society groans in man-made pains.

Very often the youth asks the question **"Why should I serve? What has society done for me except to pull me down?"** Never think that you can change the world. You cannot. Yet, **you must try to serve the world and those dependent on you, including elders and children, as best as you can. This is the way for your inner growth and mental satisfaction.**

Religious pursuit will not and cannot be a bar to perfect social and communal living. A spiritual aspirant is not to be dumb and deaf; he must be fully aware of the needs and sorrows of the world of men around him and must seek to find within himself a kindness and tolerance enough, to make his heart weep for the sorrow of others. If he has not the capacity to identify himself with his own relations and his own generation, he is not fit to enter the holy-of-holies in the temple of truth.

The spirit of sacrifice and capacity to find within oneself enough sympathy, to serve not only one's own near and dear relations but also the whole universe, thus putting their welfare first, even before one's own redemption, is one of the most important qualifications unavoidable in a true seeker.

While serving, the most important things are: **1) to keep _Narayana Bhav_, that I am serving the Lord. 2) Do not pause to question the possible fruits of the service, and 3) renounce the sense of doership... that "I am serving".**

Further reading: Why serve? by Swami Chinmayananda
On Wings and Wheels by Swami Chinmayananda, page 12
Vedanta through Letters Part 1, Old Edition
Video Cassette: Service above self: Swami Chinmayananda

Offering

Give Give Give.

1. Jan 1989

Swami Chinmayananda in a cruise liner at Virginia Beach, U.S.A. 1985.

Worldly people of
small crumpled hearts
can never understand it
and modern economics has
not dared to expound it.
Give away one
and it will be
replenished ten times.
The fish renounces
its capacity to swim
and God gives
it the capacity to hop
along as a frog. The frog
renounces that and the
running capacity is the
reward. Thus renounced
and evolved the supreme
being-man, with his
intellect and mind.
-Swami Chinmayananda.

The Gift of Time

Life is a flickering lamp kept in the stormy sea-shore of circumstances. As such **make use of every flying hour when you are young**, free and cheerful to develop your inner personality. Happiness depends on what you can give, not upon what you can get.

In life, the *giver* is the master, the receiver is always the slave. By giving, remain always a master, and decide never to be a slave! The creditor is the master, the debtor is surely a slave. The employer is the master, the employee the slave. When time employs you, you become the slave. But when you intelligently employ time, you become the master of time and time your slave!! Make a very tight programme for each day and religiously keep it up. Make a general programme for the week, and then for the month. Diligently whip yourself to be totally faithful to your own programme. Soon you will be able to programme your activities for a whole year! You will then be able to undertake an enormous volume of work and accomplish it cheerfully.

There is nothing, at any time, in any circumstances to worry over "Why this to me?" **What you have is all His gift to you. What you do with what you have is your gift to Him. Let us make Him ashamed with the glory of our gift!!**

Non Procrastination

IF I DO EVERYTHING TODAY WHAT I AM SUPPOSED TO DO TOMORROW, THEN WHAT WILL I DO ON THE LAST DAY?

Swami Chinmayananda in France. 1983.

Maya

Swami Chinmayananda in Udhampur, India.1984.

The False Glitter

Maya is defined as an inexplicable power of the Supreme, through which a delusion arises. Mirage can never be; even when we "see" the mirage waters, desert alone is the reality in it.

It is like the 'X' factor in mathematics, and its meaning is 'that which is not'. It is a jugglery of the mind.

Maya manifests in the world as three distinct, eternal qualities – *sattva*, *rajas* and *tamas*; the bright, the active and the dull. All three qualities are ever in a state of admixture.

This finite, mortal, ever changing world that we see around us, is born out of *Maya* alone. Due to non-apprehension of reality, man projects the world of objects, emotions and thoughts. Each individual creates his own world around himself due to ignorance. **Tamas** veils reality and **rajas** creates agitations in the mind. As a result of the combination of these two, we see things that are not really there, because the inner personality is poisoned by *tamas* and *rajas*. Just as when a rope is not recognized as a rope, man suffers from the misconceptions projected by his own mind that it is a serpent. When there is pure **satwa** the intellect works steadily, there is no veiling and there are no agitations. The mind is face to face with divinity. Thus, out of the stupid personality of today, a great brilliance of intelligence can be produced when the personality gets purified. This extra brilliant capacity is called **intuition**. The whole process is like an ascending spiral – it gathers momentum and carries itself.

The sense objects of the world present to us a false glitter of joy. To resist the call of this flesh, the all consuming onslaught on our senses, is the privilege and glory of man. Not knowing the art of independent living, we remain like a rudderless boat on the agitated ocean of material changes.

Just as a mariner trusts the accuracy of the compass and steers the ship of life with faith in the Scriptures, so also, the secret of success in life lies in keeping one's head above the storms of the heart.

Further reading: Vivekchoodamani verses 108 to 119
Mananam: The Mystery of Creation, pages 16 to 33

Billiards

Now I play the game on
the 'table of life' cushioned and
padded with sorrows and sobs, where
the balls roll scattered all the time and
I fun after 'my ball' with the 'cue of faith'
to push the 'jeeva' to embrace and touch all
others - either sending them to rest, at least
for a while, in the 'pockets' of peace and
joy or getting myself a few cannon strokes
pocketing after the 'contact' with
another on the table. There are six
pockets - shad is six in Sanskrit.
The 'shadanka-sadhana'
table is a thrilling
game field.

Swami Chinmayananda in Toronto, Canada. 1982.

Meet the Challenge

Life is spent in meeting challenges. You may win here and may lose there. It becomes a sport, exhausting but exhilarating, no doubt, and one can enjoy it all, if it is taken as a life-long sport.

An exhausted, sick and fatigued mind gets hit by situations, crushed by problems, mercilessly tortured by a powerful and tyrannical life. This is not because the outer life has the strength to persecute you, but you are too weak and so allow life to play havoc upon you. **Caesar would not be wolf, if Romans were not sheep.**

Be strong – not merely a physical strength of a bull – but the subtle vitality of a calm mind, replete with a will to win over all negative tendencies that poison and weaken the mind.

A strong mind is seriously cultivated by living moral values.

Further Reading: Game of Life by Swami Tejomayananda
Cassette : Transforming Anger by Swami Nikhilananda

The Technique

Swami Chinmayananda at the airport in Paris, France 1983.

They tell you to have a nice day but they do not know the technique.
If they come to the talks, they will find out 'how'!

Cultured Living ~ its technique

To "understand" truth, the mind has to be purified, unburdened, for which certain values of life are to be cultivated that will help to economize energy, which is required for a higher pursuit.

Fearlessness - Fear is generated in one whose mind is clouded by ignorance. Where there is knowledge, there is fearlessness.

Purity of heart: A dynamic religion, positive in both its theory and practice is not satisfied with a docile generation which only practises passive goodness. Members of society should burst forth with a positive glow of righteousness, bathing the entire generation with the light of truth and virtue - virtue which implies honesty of intentions and purity of motives.

Charity must come from one's sense of abundance. Unless one is able to identify oneself with others, one will not feel the noble urge to share one's possessions. Thus, charity relates to the ability to restrain one's instincts of acquisition and aggrandizement and replace them with a spirit of sacrifice.

Gifts should be given in accordance with certain ethical norms. For example, we must give only to those causes in which we believe. Charity is acceptable only when it is in agreement with our intellectual beliefs and convictions. Unless we have come to a correct and independent judgement and are convinced of the worthiness of the cause, charity should not be practised. Every benefactor has the right to inquire into the cause that he is considering patronizing.

A miserly giving will not benefit either the giver or the receiver and it is said in the Scriptures:"Having come to judge a cause as worthy, give it your entire patronage. Give in plenty, and with both hands". Also, charity must be given with modesty, avoiding feelings of egotism and vanity.

Daily study of Scriptural literature in measured quantities, provides the necessary inspiration to live a divine life. The study of the Scriptures should be more than just an intellectual exercise. We must be able to observe, analyze and understand the truth of what is being said with reference to our own lives. Regular study coupled with consistent practice gives us the strength to live in control of the sense organs. This in turn supplies us with steadiness in meditation required for realizing the Highest.

Conscious self-denial at the physical level when applied in self-development is called **austerity** *(tapas).*

The "divinely good" person is **straightforward** – upright in his thoughts, emotions and general conduct. Dishonesty has a self-destructive influence upon our personality. Actions contrary to one's own true motives result in a deceitful personality. One who lives this type of life develops a split personality and soon loses his glow of effectiveness.

Harmlessness (ahimsa) in its spiritual import means never having cruel intentions. Our intentions should never be polluted by even a trace of cruelty or hatred. Harmlessness does not consist so much in never causing physical injury as it does in never contemplating harm of any sort.

Thus, non-injury is a value of life to be applied at the level of our motives. Our motives must be non-injurious and pure. This purity of intention can arise only out of a deep sense of oneness with the Lord's creation and compassion towards all beings - good and bad alike.

Truthfulness (satyam) in its essential meaning is the attunement of our mental thoughts to our intellectual convictions, and not just giving verbal expression to our honest feelings. A disparity between thoughts and words creates a habit of " self-cancellation" of thoughts. This impoverishes our mental strength, will power and dynamism. Unless we are ready to discipline and marshal our thought-forces to the unquestioned authority of our reason, we cannot realize the unfoldment of our true and divine nature.

Absence of anger would be the ability to check waves of anger as they rise in our mind, so that anger does not manifest in our actions. It would be unnatural to think that we would never become angry. But no emotion should be allowed to overwhelm us to the extent that we cannot function properly.

In short, absence of anger does not mean without anger, but only keeping, as far as possible, an even temper.

Renunciation should not be understood as running away from life. One who tries to escape from life can never be a champion on the spiritual path. Many have hindered their spiritual unfoldment because of a misunderstanding of this word. Renunciation is not a running away from sense objects and comforts, but rather the intelligent mental attitude of detachment maintained toward the objects around us. A mere understanding of the pain-ridden nature of the world is not sufficient, however. This understanding must be completely assimilated through constant reflection and continuous realization. As we go through life's experiences with intelligent awareness, we come to an increasing understanding of the great benefits of detachment. This conviction, gathered as a result of our own personal experience, is the meaning of the term "continuous realization".

This glorious spirit of detachment cannot be practised in a sequestered place where there are no temptations or challenges. No one can learn to swim on the dry banks of a river. One must learn the art of living in this world fully and enthusiastically with a spirit of intelligent detachment.

Another quality is **absence of deviousness (unmalicious tongue)**. The ugliness or beauty of speech is determined by the personality behind it. A shattered personality will seek self-gratification in malicious gossip, whereas an inwardly harmonious person uses soft and sincere speech which echoes the fragrance of his soul. When we speak with softness of tone, clarity of expression and honesty of conviction, we bring a clear picture to the listener's mind with no veiled meanings.

To recognize the infinite beauty of life in and through all of life's imperfections is the secret of the quality of enduring tenderness, the **compassion to beings** that is found in all saints and sages. They are able to see goodness in everyone, even in the worst scoundrel.

The quality of **uncovetousness** means controlling the sense organs from excessive indulgence in sense enjoyments. The average person has an endless thirst for sense indulgence. To remain in self-control without this endless thirst is the nature of a self-disciplined person.

The conduct of such a person will be both **gentle** and **modest**. These are not so much disciplines, as they are qualities of a culturally refined individual, whose beauty and harmony become evident while contacting the world outside.

Restlessness of the mind and unsteadiness of character are reflected in the activities of an undisciplined person.The body mirrors the condition of the mind. For example, sudden outbursts of activity and exaggerated expressions of the face are all noticed in individuals who have not yet cultivated a noble character and purposeful personality. When seen in children, these may be considered to enhance their charm, but as we grow older, we realize that real beauty lies in the mastery we develop over ourselves as reflected by our actions.

Absence of fickleness. Unnecessary exhaustion through indecisive movements and thoughtless exertions are signs of a weak personality.Such individuals may be extremely imaginative, but they tend to be lacking in intellectual effectiveness and physical productivity.

Brilliance does not mean a glowing complexion produced by good food and ample rest.The glow of spirituality cannot be taken literally as a halo around one's head. It is the irresistible attraction of persons whose light or joy ever shines forth from the innermost depths of their being. It manifests in the brilliance of intellect, the twinkling joy in their eyes, the thrilling fragrance of peace around them, the serene poise in their activities, and the effulgence of their love for all. With abundant energy, they serve all and discover for themselves a fulfilment in that service.

Forbearance is not merely an ability to live patiently through the minor physical and mental inconveniences when someone injures or insults them, but the subtle boldness displayed by a person while facing the most powerful opposition and provoking situations. Weak persons often feel dejected and tempted to leave work half done when faced with many obstacles. As a result, they miss the chance to achieve their goal when victory may be just around the corner.

In order to stand firm in our convictions, we require a special energy to ward off this potential exhaustion of our mental and intellectual morale. This inner energy which arises from one's own well-integrated personality is called **fortitude**. Strong faith, consistency of purpose, a vivid perception of the ideal, and a bold spirit of sacrifice make up the source from which fortitude springs forth.

Purity is not only the inner purity of thoughts and motives, but also suggests the cleanliness of our surroundings, personal habits, and belongings. Outer cleanliness is, to a large measure, a reflection of our inner condition. Only a disciplined, cultured person can keep systematic order and cleanliness around him. One who aspires to reach perfection will automatically maintain cleanliness both in his relationship with others and his possessions. The Scriptures put great emphasis on the need for physical purity because without external purity, internal purification will be but a vague dream.

Absence of hatred means not only non-injury from the standpoint of motives, but absence of even the idea of injuring any living creature, because he knows that to harm another is to harm himself.

Absence of pride means to give up one's exaggerated notions of oneself. This relieves one immediately from many unnecessary agitations, and life becomes as light as a feather. Whereas to one who is proud, life is a heavy cross to bear.

The ethical beauty painted here is not with the purpose of giving us the idea of sending the good to an eternal heaven or damning the vicious to a perpetual hell.

Ethical virtues are the intelligent means of reviving our exhausted energy and fatigued spirit. By living these healthy values of life, we unshackle our personality from its self-made entanglements. At this moment, we are acting in accordance with the standards of the times. If we want to lift ourselves to a higher level without changing old values, a new dimension of living cannot be achieved.

Spiritual Ladder

It is easy to fall, but to climb up again takes time and effort.

Divine Life is the product of patient activity in the right direction. Everybody can make mistakes but few discover the courage to do the right thing when they discover their mistake. The fall is not bad in itself, but to rise up each time you fall needs heroism.

On the ladder of cultural growth, each step that is placed forward is an ascent towards the absolute perfection.

Spiritual Ladder

Young men never care to listen to advice. This is their nature. Nobody need curse them for it. Yet when they once trip and fall, they learn for themselves. **A serious scare is always worth more to a teenager than any amount of advice.**

But to a sincere student of Vedanta, yoga starts and is continued in self-control. To him the extreme development of his powers of concentration, through the control of his sense organs, is the greatest *tapas,* austerity.

Control of the sense organs does not mean the mere negative idea of taking our sense organs away from their sense objects. This is only half the battle. Success can be achieved when our minds are firmly fixed on the next step, in steady concentration and meditation upon the Self.

Unless he is very careful, the control gained over his senses, might at any time, get lost in the severe temptations of passing moments, especially so when he lives in the same accustomed plane of sense-objects. **Scriptures warn that it is easy even for a highly developed student of yoga, to get lost in the midst of his successes, if ever he becomes careless for a moment, as it can lead to a great fall.**

Lateral inversion

Swami Chinmayananda in Taipei, Taiwan. 1987

The reflection of a realized master is no bondage to him.
On the other hand, an ignorant man, like a bird, gets identified in its
own reflection and remains glued to it, and is caught by the bird catcher.
The world is only a reflection of Brahman having no reality apart from it.
The reflection in the mirror looks exactly like the object reflected
but there is a lateral inversion of the object
i.e., the right side looks like the left side.
Consciousness is all bliss, the world is all pain.
Brahman is perfect, the world is extremely imperfect.

Change of Vision

Once you understand that the entire world is one harmonious tapestry and that all individuals are interrelated, with each one of us having certain responsibilities and duties to society, then you will no longer ask: "Why should I feel responsible for my neighbour?". You will naturally feel extremely interested and responsible because your neighbour is not someone different from you. There should be oneness in our life and in our endeavour, which can only happen when we rise to a new dignity within ourselves.

Your neighbour's job and his attitudes are all different from you, just as your leg is different from your hand. Yet, are they both not yours?

If you understand this idea, then you will see the whole universe as one mighty expression of the divine spark of existence.

The universe is a cosmos and not a chaos; there exists a mental affinity, a scientific law, a rhythm of mental relationship in which the entire living world is held together, in one web of love. To assume differences in the world is to belie this great oneness in life.

Seek him in the smile of your friends, in the glow of the angry eyes, in the throb of love, in the storms of passion. Everywhere it is his glow that is gleaming through different emotions, thoughts and actions. Seek him in the thrill of the dawn, in the sadness of the dusk, in the embrace of rains, in the hustling storms, in the murmuring breeze — in green pastures, in the blue lotus, in the confluence of the graceful Ganges and the restless Yamuna. He is everywhere — in everything — not with mortal legs and hands, but in his presence as the divine joy infinite. **You are in him — you are but he alone.**

Further reading: Atma Bodha by Swami Chinmayananda
The Holy Geeta: Chapter 10 and 11
Mananam:The Mystery of Creation,
explanation of Lateral Inversion page 17

Short Cut!

Further reading:
The Holy Geeta commentary by Swami Chinmayananda chapter 17 verse 2 & 3

Faith

Blind faith is not for a thinker. Mere superstitious religiosity is a morass out of which the victim can never be redeemed. It is far easier to bring light to the path of an honestly intelligent atheist.

Faith does not mean an idle intellectual surrender, or any unquestioned sentimental and emotional tribute at the altar of a symbol or idea, which one does not understand. Faith is a psychological and intellectual understanding and balance, without which not even our common day to day business of life can, in fact, be efficiently transacted. Faith in ourselves and in our capacities is the nucleus of all achievements. If a man has lost all faith in himself, he turns hysterical in constitution. In this sense of the term, we must have faith in the spiritual science too, in our instructor, and above all, a faith in ourselves that we will be able to live the great and noble values of life.

Faith in each man takes the hue and quality from the stuff of his being – the predominant temperament in him. The essence of faith lies in the secret energy of the ego with which it holds on to its convictions, to reach a definite chosen end by well thought out and entirely self-planned means.

Faith itself is of three kinds: the divine, the undivine and the diabolic, and this in turn commands our view in life. An individual's physical activities, psychological behaviour and intellectual make-up are all ordered by the type of faith he has come to maintain in himself. If the faith is of the wrong type, the entire expression of his personality in all walks of life and in every field of endeavour can only be ugly. The temperaments that rule the behaviour and faith of the human are three in number - the good **(sattvic),** the passionate **(rajasic)** and the dull (**tamasic**).

Faith in Vedanta means the ability to digest mentally and comprehend intellectually, the full import of the advice of the saints and the declarations of the Scriptures.**It is said that faith is the belief in what we do not know, so that we come to know what we believe in.**

Under His Wings

In case a Guru takes you under his wings to guide you and protect you - it is a great blessing.

Swami Chinmayananda in Philadelphia, U.S.A. 1985.

The constant mental awareness of the Ideal through the person of the Guru steadily raises the moral tempo of the student, which would otherwise take long years to develop.

The Grace of a Teacher

Many are the stories in our *Puranic* treasure houses, which indicate how even a passing word of a great master has come true in the end. There is nothing strange in it. It ought to be so. When a radio is tuned to Delhi, and if that radio sings, it cannot but be the songs sung in the Delhi broadcasting room. A radio is incapable of making its own noises. Similarly, a God-man, who, in his realized Self-perfection, has totally tuned himself to That, will not and cannot express himself in words futile. **All his thoughts are the thoughts of the total-mind.** His words are always the immutable words of the divine will. This ought to be the intelligent understanding of every disciple, if he is to profit from the grace of a guru in the spiritual field.

It does not mean that all you have to do is to meet the guru, and thereafter he will carry you like a mule to the goal. The guru is like a gardener that will nurture the student, but the blossoming, the real fragrance, must come from within.

Prostration

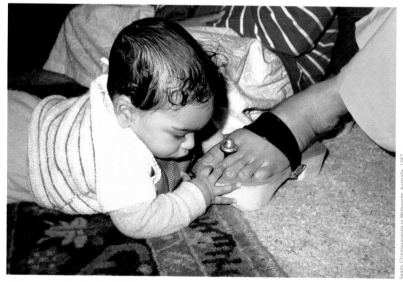

Swami Chinmayananda in Melbourne, Australia, 1987.

The shoes of a Vedantic Master should always be kept shining; then when the student prostrates, what will he see there? Himself! By prostrating what goes out of us is our ego!

Guru - shishya Parampara

Swami Tapovanam with disciple Swami Chinmayananda at Tapovan Kuti in Uttarkashi.1956. Photograph by Swami Sunderananda

The "young" with his dynamism, may serve the world. It is only the "old" with his wisdom alone, that can "reach" the truth.

"young" = spiritually young

The Legacy

When a perfect teacher and a perfect student come together, it is not a physical meeting but a harmonious understanding between the teacher and the taught that is to be cultivated. The teacher gets to know the student's beauty and his ugliness in between the student's questions and his service. What should be the mental attitude of the student towards the teacher – love, respect or fear? He considers the teacher as the Lord himself – and an intimate relationship, like a blood relationship, that of a kith and kin develops.

A seeker approaches a master and pours out his question on life and seeks to understand the logic of the happenings in life. The answers given by sympathetic masters in their hermitages, on the banks of the Ganga, are all traditionally handed down to us and they constitute the books of Hindu philosophy.

The entire science of the spirit preserved through memory, was handed down from a generation of masters, to a generation of disciples and they to their disciples, and it is called the Veda_s. In this process, as a river that gathers more and more water from its tributaries, the tradition grew in bulk and details. As each generation got the heritage from the elders at each period, new details clarifying the same fundamental truth were added to it. The text remained the same, but the explanations were original.

The entire literature was handed down by gurus to their disciples by word of mouth and the students had to preserve it in their memory. It worked well so long as the pre-occupation of living was not too severe. But when population and pressures increased, Hinduism was facing a danger of total annihilation.

It is at such a crucial juncture in our spiritual history, that we find the advent of the great revolutionary reformer, the poet-philosopher, **Vyasa.** He retrieved life giving gems of wisdom, the Vedic passages, and for the first time edited them into

continued.....

The *guru-shishya parampara,* shown here as flowing down from its original source, the Lord, in the form of Gyana-Ganga, the flow of knowledge, meandering down through the saints and sages—Veda Vyasa, Adi Sankara and his four disciples...
Then, Swami Tapovanam, Swami Chinmayananda and Swami Tejomayananda.

four written volumes, which constitute today, the four great Vedas of the Hindus - the **Rig Veda,** the **Yajur Veda,** the **Sama Veda** and the **Atharva Veda.** Each book contains three sections: 1) **Mantras** 2) **Brahmanas** 3) **Upanishads.** The Upanishads are found in the last section of each Veda and therefore the philosophy of the Upanishads has come to be otherwise called as **Vedanta** — the end of Veda.

The theme of the Vedas is the infinite and the eternal. Beyond the purview of the **waking, dream** and **deep sleep** states lies stretched the soft world of bliss and beatitude, where **the finite mortal rediscovers himself to be of the stature of God, the infinite.**

The language of the market place, the words of the drawing room, the phrases of the slums, the slang of the drinking booth, can never hope to express the perfect and the immortal. Language cannot define or even vaguely report upon the transcendental experience, which one comes to live in the stillness of one's own mind.

In the Vedas, truth is not **described.** It is only **indicated,** hence the necessity of a seeker to be at the feet of a sympathetic master, who lives the perfection with every moment.

Further reading: Aitrareya Upanishad, Introduction by Swami Chinmayananda

Love Story

Swami Chinmayananda at the Dal Lake, Srinagar, Kashmir. 1984.

All my life is the story of my love for Him. I must have spoken, in all, a dozen words out of fear born of respect.

(Swami Chinmayananda in reference to Swami Tapovanam, his Guru.)

Reverence

Where our sense of love from the mind and our sense of respect from the intellect merge together, the attitude so generated at the **confluence** of **love** and **respect** is called *reverence.* We may love without respect; we may also respect a person without loving him. For example, most people love children, but they need not respect children. Almost all children respect their teachers, but they may not love all the teachers. Thus it can be seen that reverence is generated and maintained only by an integrated mind-intellect.

Thus, when we have a deep sense of reverence for life and for all living creatures, then alone does our love for others become potent. Someone may love us, but in case they have no respect for us, we will surely feel insulted for all their sincere and loving approaches. **The lover must have a subtle sense of reverence toward the beloved.** If we love our parents, but have no reverence for them, they will not be influenced by our love.

Loving the world without reverence for life and people is like preparing curry, finely cooked and cleanly served, but without salt!

Therefore, if the love for the Lord is without the recognition of his infinitude, which is the essence of the Lord, it will be such a self-insulting relationship that it cannot mature into the ecstasy of true devotion.

Electricity–Yoga

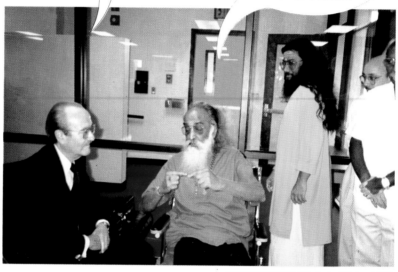

Swami Chinmayananda at Washington D.C. airport. 1991.

Shut up your mind and get out of this prison of matter.
Unveil from the BMI, the raiments of vasanas, and embrace the Self.
By putting your finger into the socket like this.......
will explain to you what is electricity.
Similarly, you can never understand that State
unless you experience it for yourself.

Further Reading:Vedanta through letters Part I, question on Puranic gods
Lord Krishna by Swami Chinmayananda ;   The Holy Geeta: chapter XII;
Hindu Culture by Swami Tejomayananda;   Art of God Sybolism by Swami
Chinmayananda; The Glory of Ganesh by Swami Chinmayananda;
Glory of Mother by Swami Chinmayananda

Mystical Literature

In India, we do not have mythology at all. We have only 'mystic symbolism'. It is a unique literature. The west does not have this literature.The nearest is the mythology of the Greeks and Romans. So they called it Hindu mythology.

The hasty reader discards traditional beliefs and stories as mythological absurdities. They do not recognize the *language of symbolism.* The stories look fantastic, but when the symbolism is understood, one will appreciate the great wisdom of the Rishis, for **packing an entire philosophy in unforgettable pieces of literature.**

This idea is dramatized in the mischief of the Blue Boy of *Vrindavan*. He steals the clothes of the milk-maids in mischief. A low mentality of sensuality, steeped in the philosophy of the flesh, when it enters this haven of joyous mystic symbolism can only enjoy the superficial meaning. The idea is to reach the Lord in utter nakedness. Wrapped up in the clothes of *vasanas,* you cannot reach there.The same was meant by Jesus, when he said that it is easier for a camel to go through the eye of a needle, than for a rich man (rich in *vasanas*) to enter the gates of heaven.

Puranic literature is not only to be read as a history or a biography. It is written in the style of the Vedas – mystic style. **It is a song of the soul's adventure to rediscover itself.** Veda Vyasa, a Vedic teacher, a master mind, a man of realization – when he took the pen, in his maturity, he did not do so only for writing a love story or a novel. Krishna is painted throughout as Sri Krishna Paramatman. Story by story, incident by incident, the canvas reveals a word-picture of **the science of self-mastery;** the spiritual self-development – both in theory and practice.

Let us undress and enter the eternal flow that sweeps from the rishis. Let us in abandon play in its cool waters. Who knows? Let us not look back. Let the Yellow Robe steal away our clothes. In shameless nakedness, in the divine nudity of heart, we shall approach him on the tree of life and beg for our raiment. **In the sanctified robes, we shall live ever in the ecstasy of his touch.**

To the Ego in Man

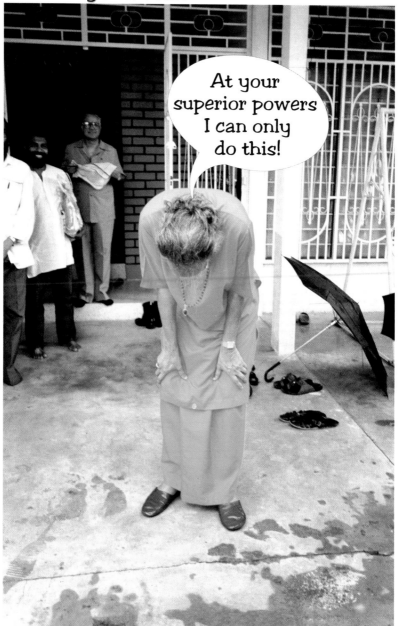

To a devotee who put her own interpretation on his words.

Swami Chinmayananda in Kuala Lumpur, Malaysia. 1989.

The Ego

Ego is not a noun, but a verb. It is nothing but a bundle of past actions and reactions. It is only a record of actions and reactions, from birth until now. Throw this stinking bundle down and look at the world without this muddy poison. Where it is dropped, divine experience arises.

We generally get agitated due to the pulls of success and failure. On the rising tide of success, our ego dances in a vain joy, while in the hollows of failures, it feels miserable and crushed. Ego is a false identification with our body, mind and intellect. When the ego is divinized, the individual will automatically remain equanimous in both success and failure.

The internal apparatus of a human being is a conglomeration of the **mind, intellect, ego** and **memory.** The four together are called ***antahkarana.***

Happy in Life?

Swami Chinmayananda and Swami Tejomayananda in U.S.A. 1986. Photograph by Michael Maysel.

Alone but not Lonely

Aloneness is different from loneliness. By remaining lonely at a place where there is nobody else, realization is not guaranteed. Even in the midst of a crowd you can be "alone" in Brahman, the One without a second. Aloneness is not in the surroundings, but it is in one's attitude of remaining with all attention fixed upon that one goal, *eka-antam.* The habit of constantly remaining alone, even in a busy market place is to be cultivated. **Learn to sit down for at least ten minutes every day without any activity, physical or mental.** Without expectation of possible enjoyments, cultivate the habit of remaining alone, remembering God.

A young man has to pour out his best, in order to build up his life. This needs constant vigilance and meaningful self-application, which is a drain on his intellectual stamina. This can be exhausting and weakening, unless he regularly replenishes the brain drain and replaces the mental wastage. **In quietude, our mind can bring forth for us, ideas, ideals, solutions, remedies, original thoughts and endless creative ideas.**

At such moments of inner tranquility, the mind can reach out to thoughts profound, which are ordinarily too high for us to readily grasp in the sweep of our personal understanding. **When we are still and our mind is quiet, then alone the infinite resources of the total-mind will flow down to flood our within.** Then meditation becomes a true education, a secret preparation of ourselves to face the world of changing circumstances.

Meditation can make of an ordinary man, an incomparable genius. Scientists, artists, men of action - have climbed to the peak of their individual achievement in life, during such accidental moods of inspiration and unearthly spontaneity. A man of realization fears none, and so, nothing can threaten him. We run after the world of objects because we have the desire to enjoy them. He has none, for he is ever content and joyous. **In his wisdom he is an exemplar, and yet, humble enough to maintain an equal vision for all.**

To the youth in Hong Kong

Don't go to the Peak to meditate; reach the 'Peak' in meditation!

Swami Chinmayananda in Hong Kong, 1987.

Meditation

Meditation is not meant for beginners. In meditation one is wingless, if one has not acquired a decent share of concentration-power and a perfect knowledge of how to fix the mind at will, on a single point for some length of time. Therefore, *japa,* or repeating the Lord's name, is recommended in the beginning. Beginners must strive to make the mind and intellect quiet, calm, serene, single-pointed and sincere. This can be achieved in your daily activities, by performing them with care and attention. **Be a mirror! Reflect everything; keep nothing. No matter what passes in front of the mirror, no image remains.**

When we meditate upon that which is entertaining and pleasant to us, our mind, in its gathering joy and satisfaction, quietens itself and the outgoing thoughts become steadily rooted in contemplation. **Thus the poets in their poetic moods, scientists in their laboratory, artisans at their work - all of them discover a joy that is not typical of what we usually experience in the mind.** This joy arises subjectively from the steadiness of the mind.

However steady the mind may become, and even gets filled with the noblest thoughts, the mind still exists. This mind veils the Self by a curtain of thought-agitations. Through steady meditation upon the Self, the mental projections and consequent experiences of the worlds of waking, dream and deep sleep, get rolled up and burned in the fire of Self-realization. This realization is to be achieved by each one of us, all by ourselves, in ourselves, for ourselves. We need to note modes of living conducive to these attempts at self-evolution, as they constitute the spiritual values. **At the highest peak of divine life stands the mighty temple of meditation.** In your climb towards it, hasten slowly...

In the hushed silence of inspired joy, in the roaring laughter of silent meditation, in the motionless dance of ecstasy, in the freezing heat of *tapas,* he whispers his deafening message: **"I am you, you are me".**

Further Reading: Meditation and Life by Swami Chinmayananda
Art of Contemplation by Swami Chinmayananda

I am Unborn!

Age? Blab! I am unborn! The older they consider me, the nearer they are to the truth.

Swami Chinmayananda, 4 months old, "born" in Ernakulam, Kerala, India 1916.

Further reading:

Journey of a Master (biography of Swami Chinmayananda) by Nancy Patchen
Swami Chinmayananda – A life of Inspiration and Service by Rudite Emir
Ageless Guru by Radhika Krishna Kumar
At Every Breath – a teaching by Rudite Emir
Mandukya Upanishad, commentary by Swami Chinmayananda
– Chapter III verse 27, 28.
Dakshinamurthy Strotram: verse 2

The Unborn, the Undying

(Swami Chinmayananda's letter to a college student, who had requested Swamiji to send his bio-data)

Blessed Self,

Hari Om!
I was born in Kerala, brought up in the North, hardened in Punjab, softened in Uttarkashi, criticized everywhere, applauded in some places, but accepted and worshipped by everyone.
I am a riddle to myself. Prattling was my profession and preaching is my job now. Everywhere I earned a lot and squandered it all over the community. I am by training a religious man, by experience a Vedantin, by inclination a *bhakta*, by temperament a *karma yogi*, in practice an integral *yogi*.
My faith is in democracy, I am convinced by socialism and I am committed to the impossible theory of 'love-all'. Thick-skinned and hard boned, I have a mail of laughter to cover and protect both my head and heart. So, stabs do not penetrate me, spears cannot cleave me, whippings do not lash me. I eat and drink, take regular bath and sleep, wear clothes but no matted hair. I work for eighteen to nineteen hours a day, preach the rest of the time.
You can meet me easily in my books or in the *pooja* room of any man, be he a Hindu, a Christian or a Muslim. The white man adores me, the yellow man recognizes me, the brown man worships me, and the black man loves me.

With Prem and Om.
CHINMAYANANDA

The Self is considered as the most ancient, *purana,* ageless, because the eternal truth is that which was before all creation; which remains the same all through the ages of existence and which shall ever remain the same even after the projections of plurality have ended. 'Oldest' or 'ancient' indicates the one Self, that provides a substratum even for the concept of time. **The Self is never born even at the birth of the body. It was already there to illumine that experience.**

The Self can only remain unborn and changeless. In case we accept that something has come out of reality as an effect, then we will have to enquire - what caused the cause from which the perceived effect itself has come. If we accept the causation in the supreme, then we cannot come to 'the first cause,' which is in itself uncaused. Such an unending muddle of causation hunting will catch us and drown us in a welter of *regress ad infinitum.*

"Say Cheese!"

Swami Chinmayananda in Taipei, Taiwan. Photograph by Madhuri Jhala

Brahman, when clicked with the mind-intellect camera,
not focused properly, or if shaken even a bit with the agitations
of desires, will come to snap in but the ugly *samsar*. But if you
have *vivek, vairagya, shad sampatti, mumukshatvam,* then ...

this is That!

*A photo is just a shadow of a moment caught and frozen for
ever. That which indicates a subtle truth with its gross form,
is an idol.*

The Supreme Brahman

The Atman, or the life-centre, is a motionless entity, but seems to be moving only when it is conditioned by the mind and functioning as its manifestations, as thought waves.

A stress in consciousness is a thought. **A flow of thoughts is what is known as the mind.** A continuous stream of thoughts maintained in our bosom, provides us with a delusory expression of the mighty and powerful mind. **Through the mind we see the world of names and forms projected upon consciousness.** Thus the perceived objects and the perceiving equipment are all 'stresses' in consciousness. When the illusion-creating, delusion-breeding 'stresses' are relinquished, through deep meditation, the thoughts cease; the mind is lifted, and the hallucination of the universe rolls away.

When ten pieces of iron, of different shapes, are put into the fire and removed only after they are red-hot, they appear as the cubical-fire, rectangular-fire, triangular fire, elliptical fire, etc. The fire itself has no shape, but takes the shape of the iron pieces.

Similarly, the light of consciousness appears to function according to the modifications of the equipments. Sunlight itself has no shape. But it takes the shape of the waves, the ripples and the bubbles in the sea. Its shape depends on the object it illumines at any given time.

When consciousness illumines the experiences of the mind, it seems to gather to itself the attitude of the enjoyer. When it illumines the activities of the world outside, it appears to take the attitude of the doer. ***In fact, it is not involved in anything.*** When it appears to be so, it is but an illusion. The Self does not move; **motion is a change in time and space**. The word *motionless* refers to that which is beyond time and space; it is only an indication of the all pervasiveness of Brahman, the supreme reality, in terms of existence and consciousness.

Further reading: Commentary on Vivekchoodamani by Swami Chinmayananda
Isavasya Upanishad: verse 4

Hold the thoughts!

The space between two thoughts is the underlying Consciousness.

Mind the Gap

Between every two bogies of a train there is a gap. So also, between two thoughts there is always the underlying consciousness.

Who is the seer in me? Is it the body? Or can it be the mind? Or is it the intellect? Who illumines for me my hopes, fears, likes, dislikes, joys, pains, loves, hatreds, passions, anger etc.? Enquire.

Infinite consciousness is the screen on which the hero and heroine are dancing. The white screen is immaculate, unmoving, on which alone the moving shadows can give the story.

In the same way, are you not seeing things and beings moving? What supports them? What is the substratum? The movie was on the screen. Without the screen – no movie. What is it without which, nothing can exist? That substratum that supports is consciousness. **Movement or change can be perceived only against a motionless background.** But you are not aware of that. Your attention is on the movie... the constant change of names and forms, projected out by the rushing thoughts of your mind.

But...
When the film breaks... Ah... The screen is seen. Have you ever heard of any one silent at that time? Similarly, the thunder of realisation, when the substratum – the pure consciousness, is 'seen'!!! Ha! Hu! Ha Hu Ha Huuuuuuu.......

Further reading: Meditation & Life by Swami Chinmayananda
                  Art of Contemplation by Swami Chinmayananda
                  Taittiriya Upanishad commentary by Swami Chinmayananda
                  Kena Upanishad commentary by Swami Chinmayananda

Who realizes the Truth?

Swamiji! When vasanas get exhausted, then the ego is not there. Then who realizes?

There is an ant fallen inside this cake. He looks to the right and finds there is cake. On top of him and below him is cake; it is all cake-o-cake. The intellect is like the ant!

Swami Chinmayananda in Taipei, Taiwan, 1987.

Like a salt doll dropped into the ocean disappears to become the ocean, so also the ego realizes that "I do not exist" and disappears to become the Self.

Further reading: Atma Bodha pages 65, 66, 67.
Mandukya Karika: Advaita Prakarana verse 33.
Katha Upanishad

Who realizes the Truth?

When a seeker succeeds in removing all the veils of ignorance, which are nothing but his own mental agitations caused by the clouding of his intellect, the self-effulgent Self spontaneously reveals itself in its own light. Meaning, it does not come as a result of any deliberate action, but **is a spontaneous revelation, as though by the intervention of divine grace.** The feverish play of our restless mind has set this divine power in us at naught! This dormant faculty will be aroused in one who *consciously* transcends his mind and intellect. **Thereafter, the meditator is guided along the road to the sanctum sanctorum of truth by this pure power to-know-the-knowledge itself.** This state is beyond the realm of language, beyond the mind and intellect. Contemplative power alone can apprehend the reality. This apprehension is not an objective experience. It is an uncompromising and total "becoming". **This intuitive power is nothing other than a mind turned inward and held at attention.**

At the boundaries of the finite world of matter, all languages stop. Beyond them only the language of the soul, silent meditation, is available for the spirit to converse with the spirit. As at dawn, the darkness rolls off and the light of its own glory brings everything to our cognition, so too, at the dawn of wisdom, all knowledge bursts up to our awareness.

The spirit overwhelms and conquers the realms of the mind and the moment of conquest of matter by the spirit is the moment of Self-realization. At the moment of recognition of the subject by the subject, there is no object other than the subject to observe. **When the mind and intellect are transcended, the individual-self rediscovers its identity with the total Self.** And peeping over its own limitations, *as it were*, comes face to face with the eternal Self; and when thus, the highly evolved ego comes to reflect the light of the eternal knowledge, the reflection merges itself *in-a-process-of-knowing* to become one with the Self. Seeing the reflection in a mirror, we do not actually come to know so much of the reflection, as through it, we come to understand the source of the reflection, our own face.

At the Portal of Truth

Come!
I am waiting
for you!

Swami Chinmayananda in Bali, 1986. Photograph by Kamal Daswani.

People would ask Swami Chinmayananda "Are you realized?"
He would say "I am waiting for you at the Gate. We will all enter together!"

To one who has the temperament to seek life, the anxiety to realize perfection, the daring to follow the foot prints of the seers of the world, the courage to live the moral and ethical values, the heroism to barter one's all to achieve the highest – such a one is not a 'mineral man' nor a 'vegetable man' nor an 'animal man' - but he is the noblest creation under the sun, a perfect 'man-man', standing right in front of the door of truth, demanding as a **'God-man'** his admission into the sanctum-sanctorum!

No amount of scriptural study is of any avail.

Fulfill the reading with meditation. Through meditation, crawl up to the arena of joy and peace. There in the Topmost Tower we shall meet, away from all disturbances.

Come.

I am waiting for you.

LETTER TO A 21 YEAR OLD

SWAMI CHINMAYANANDA

Hari Om! Salutations!

Today you are 21: a full grown responsible young man ready to make or mar your life. Live straight, and pleasant & cheerful, serving others as much as you can — not for their applause, but for your satisfaction and joy.

I wish you all success.

Jai Jai Sarveswara!

Letter to Jujhar Singh (name deleted from letter)

126

Vision of Life

Your study and work must bring to your recognition the larger vision of life, the wider vision of existence.

Swami Chinmayananda talking to the youth in Kuala Lumpur, Malaysia. 1987

Youth - Your Future

The youth are at a stage where they can mould history. All revolutionary changes for progress have been made by the youth. **But in order to do this, they must know history**; the mistakes made and the changes brought about in the past. They must have the knowledge, the right judgment and the capacity to plan. The old gang of cronies and bandicoots who had been wielding power would neither allow them to change anything, nor could they themselves do anything new.

The old will follow the old orthodox methods; lacking the capacity to absorb changes, they can naturally neither see new ideas, nor implement them. Their interest lies in maintaining the status quo in whichever field they are in - religion, science, politics or whatever - and thus stagnation sets in. If the youth follow orthodoxy slavishly and do not carve out new possibilities, they are doomed to frustration and then to escapism; excessive indulgence in physical and mental exertion. **They try to exhaust themselves in wasteful dissipation of physical, mental, psychological and intellectual energy – smoking, drinking, drugs and loud noisy music.**

Is there a way out? The answer is that they have to go through planned study. It is not enough only to imbibe what is given by the media, because that is not knowledge, but modulated propaganda. They must learn to judge for themselves from their own convictions and then have the courage to live upto them. Their plans and vision must come from within, based on their own **understanding** of the world, their **patriotism**, love for society and loyalty to the country, not necessarily to the government.

Even one such leader can bring about a great change. **Youthful vigour and intelligence must not be allowed to go into the wrong direction.**

The present has been created by the past, and the future will come out of the present. Unless the youth of today are vigilant, dynamic and smart, the nation, and with it, their future, will sink. continued....

All powerful governments become tyrannical, as supreme power corrupts supremely. Youth have the power to vote, the power to choose their leaders. They do not have to blindly follow the politicians; rather they should lead the politicians by the nose, which is true democracy. Till now, they have not thought for themselves, they have not cultivated social awareness; they have not generated political consciousness.

The youth have to get geared up to work, to acquire, and having acquired, to distribute – for a healthy nation. **Corruption, the naked display of selfishness in cancerous personalities will go only when the youth opposes it;** not by goondaism, the noisy mobism of the universities, or the guns of the terrorists, but by organized disciplined planning and the courage of conviction in implementing these plans.

First, acquire knowledge, judge for yourself, then learn to sit together to take decisions, to carve out the future. You must get inspired by an ideal or an altar and then dedicate yourself to it. This altar need not be religious. It may be professional, social, economic. Whatever your field, excel in it and give it your best. **You must take the nation to a new sunrise but not with guns; it is no enemy that we have to fight.**

When Gandhiji said that he was planning to launch a non-violent movement, people laughed at him. Even on the salt-making march, he was alone when he set out. By the time he crossed a few villages, a big crowd joined him, some out of curiosity and others because of the herd instinct. A crowd of newspersons came to watch him. By the time he reached Bombay, all those who had laughed at him were slaves in adoration at his feet.

Somebody has to start, and you are being given the chance, which no other generation in recent times has got in our country. You are standing on the threshold of your collapse or your revival. This needs an enormous self-respect, love and reverence for your country.

Unless you are inspired by an ideal and unless you know the glory of the past, how will you draw inspiration? An orphan who does not know who to call his own, may loot or steal; but on the other hand, a person who knows his father and mother and the tradition of the family, will act only in a constructive way, so as not to dishonour that family. **The quality of one's behaviour will depend upon the respect one has for the institution, community, nation or religion to which one belongs.**

Our education system is so wrong. History has no place in it. **Without knowing the glory of the country, how can one love the country?** Don't wait for the political parties to do it for you. Leave them alone. Study hard as much as you can, develop your mind and intellect and pour it out for rebuilding the country.

The leader should keep this in mind at all times: the illiterate masses, who listen to the thundering eloquence of the leaders on platforms, may not often understand the full import of their ideals, but they feel and appreciate the behaviour and attitude of the leaders in society. **These millions copy the decorum, set as a standard by the leaders, not by their words but by their actions.** And we know that these millions constitute the country. Thus rebuilding of a society or a country can be achieved only through the integrated character of its leaders.

Have a vast vision. From the Himalayas to Cape Comorin, it is my country. **Everyone is my brother, be he a Christian or a Muslim.** In India, there are only two societies: those who *were* Hindus and those who *are* Hindus. India is a wonderful country, culturally beautiful, spiritually strong and geographically blessed. What a variety of people we are – and one bond is keeping us together: the bond of Hinduism, like a string holding a row of pearls. **The young people of today must rise to the call and do their duty to get this great nation on the move again;** not by disintegrating and destroying – no progress is possible that way – but by bringing the glory of our cultural consciousness out in the beauty of their actions.

Gratitude

I have tried my best to impart what I had gained from **my beloved teachers**, to thousands around the world. This work has been my sport, my mission in life. You have all helped me always. We shall meet in our hearts. May Sri Jagadeeshwara bless us always.

When will I see you again?

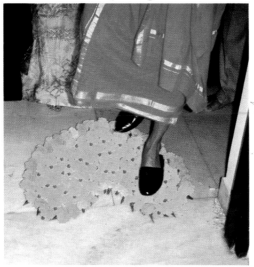

Swami Chinmayananda in Ahmedabad, India, 1993.

Whenever you shut your eyes and look within, you will find me in your heart.